EQ FITNESS HANDBOOK

You In Relationship

300 Daily Practices to build EQ Fitness

By Jan Johnson

Learning in Action Technologies
www.learninginaction.com

Library of Congress Cataloging-in-Publication Data

Johnson, Jan, 2010.

EQ fitness handbook: you in relationship—300 daily
practices to build EQ fitness

ISBN 978-0-578-04591-7

1. Emotional Intelligence 2. Personal Development

Printed in the United States of America

For further information on Emotional Intelligence or
purchase of additional fitness handbooks:
Call 206-299-2360 or email liat@learninginaction.com

TABLE OF CONTENTS

Introduction

By our very nature, we are emotional beings. We come into this world fully wired as emotional, social beings ready to learn, grow, and prosper in relationships. Developing emotional intelligence, however, is a learned process that begins at birth and continues throughout our lives.

Emotional intelligence includes the ability to be self-aware of our own emotions, to be conscious of the emotions of the people around us, and to manage our own emotions effectively in our relationships, even when those relationships become difficult. Developing greater emotional intelligence and managing ourselves and our relationships effectively is a lifetime learning process for all of us. When we are comfortable and under little stress, most of us enjoy life and our relationships. When we are faced with conflict and stress, however, most of us move to protect our emotional well being in ways learned early in our lives. Some of these learned responses are life-giving and serve us well as adults, while others may have helped us maneuver in relationships when we were children but interfere with our achieving effective and satisfying professional and personal relationships as adults.

The good news is that we are not condemned to endlessly repeat ineffective or unhealthy responses throughout our lives: research shows that the neuroplasticity of our brains allows us to learn new ways to react internally and to interact with others. Through highly focused, disciplined practice, we can make radical and profound changes in our emotional reactions and our lives.

This handbook is written for individuals who are serious about their own development and want to make a targeted, focused effort to build the core dimensions of their Emotional Intelligence (EQ) and thereby enhance their capacity to enjoy a wide range of relationships. It offers a brief description of each of the three core capacities that characterize emotional intelligence—Self-Reflection, Empathy, and Self-Regulation—and specific practices that can be incorporated into our daily lives to increase our emotional intelligence in different key dimensions. Its ultimate purpose is to build EQ fitness and thereby increase your awareness and choices in the midst of difficult relationships or challenging situations.

To use this book effectively, select one or two areas for development from your EQ In Action Profile report or from feedback you have received from 360 feedback tools, friends, colleagues, or other sources. For example, if you wish to increase your empathy or your level of optimism or to better manage fear, you can turn to the table of contents to find specific chapters or practices that may help you accomplish those goals. If you have not taken the EQ In Action Profile, you may want to start this process by taking the brief survey in Appendix B, which will help you identify some lifelong relationship patterns that may be keeping you from being as successful at managing yourself and interacting with others as you would like. The findings of this survey can help guide you in selecting an area of development for yourself and some specific practices that you can add to your daily living.

You will find that some of the same practices are repeated in different sections of the handbook because they are highly relevant to more than one dimension of emotional intelligence. You will also notice that more than half of the chapters offer practices for building self-awareness, as this capacity is central to understanding and improving our emotional intelligence. Therefore I encourage you to include at least some of the practices in those chapters as part of your development plan.

Building emotional fitness can be transformational! Like any other fitness program, however, it will take disciplined practice, so keep your eye on the prize and use your coach, friends, or family for support. Best wishes on your Fitness Program.

ACKNOWLEDGEMENTS

This handbook is a revision and expansion of the original handbook published in 2004. The use of the handbook by coaches, educators, and consultants over the years has been rewarding and has offered guidance for this expanded version The added years of learning in working with clients have added richness to the content of this handbook.

A special thanks and appreciation to Dave Erb, PhD, for providing the conceptual framework for our EQ In Action Profile and to Ron Short, PhD, for the guidance his thirty years in working with Self in Relationship has provided to our work and this handbook. Thanks also to Jeannine Hall for her contribution in serving clients day to day and offering her own experience and insights into the creation of this handbook.

Thanks to the coaching clients who generously offered their time to review the draft of this handbook and gave specific feedback. These clients include Barbara Bannon, Mary Eshenko, Art Haines, Bonnie Hovel, Molly Kaufman, Marie MacDonald, Patsi Maroney, Elaine Millam, Kristie McLean, Dorothy Moga, Genevieve Moore, Beth Page, Kathy Taberner, and Mary Utley. My goal was to make this handbook as useful as possible for our coaches' clients and for any adult wanting to further their development as a leader and as an effective human being

Thanks to the many practitioners, theorists, and scholars whose half-century of exciting work brings depth to our understanding and focus to the "daily practices" presented in this handbook. We are continually learning and refining our efforts to create powerful, effective practices that make a real difference.

Thanks to my patient editor, Jeanne Barker-Nunn, PhD, who has brought freshness and clarity to this writing. I relied on her talent every step of the way. Thanks also to Glen Iwasaki for his graphic design of the handbook.

I appreciate being a part of this immense discipline called emotional and social intelligence that is now being embraced by individuals and organizations world-wide as a critical piece in building leadership talent and increasing overall performance in the organization.

Jan Johnson, *President*
Learning In Action Technologies
206-299-2360
http://learninginaction.com

CHAPTER 1

Emotional Intelligence and Its Key Dimensions

We should take care not to make the intellect our god; it has,
of course, powerful muscles,
but no personality. It cannot lead; it can only serve.

— Albert Einstein

Emotions are at the root of everything we do, the unquenchable origin
of every act more complicated than reflex. In all cases, emotions are
humanity's motivator and its omnipresent guide.

— Thomas Lewis, *A General Theory of Love*

We live in exciting times. With the advent of new non-invasive technologies, researchers from a number of disciplines have been making unprecedented discoveries about how our brain functions and develops, about how we process and respond to information and emotions. As a result, we have increasing evidence that emotions are the ultimate driver of everything we do and that by becoming conscious of those emotions, we can actually shape how our brains respond to them. In other words, being aware in the moment of our emotional experience can help us make effective and satisfying choices about our actions and attitudes.

Based in large part on these new insights, Daniel Goleman, other psychologists, and neuroscientists began to study what Goleman has termed

Emotional Intelligence (EQ). Among the findings revealed by this new research are the following:

- Emotional Intelligence is more important than IQ in achieving professional and personal success in our lives.

- Emotional Intelligence is the primary determinant of the quality of our relationships, at work and in our personal lives.

- Emotional Intelligence is developed and sustained through our interactions with others.

- Emotional Intelligence can be developed throughout our lives through disciplined, focused practice and can radically improve the quality of our lives.

Through this and earlier research, we know that the development of Emotional Intelligence begins at birth and in the context of our earliest relationships, and that its core capacities are in place by the age of four. These core capacities—Self-Reflection, Empathy, and Self-Regulation—are central to the development of the self and undergird our ability to be functioning, capable human beings in the world. Thus understanding how our brains develop in relationship can provide valuable guidance for intentionally building EQ in children and adults. We now know that the neuroplasticity of our brains allows them to literally restructure themselves in response to the demands placed on them. As Sharon Begley points out in Train Your Mind, Change Your Brain, "use it or lose it" is an apt description of how our brains function. Understanding this process can allow us to intentionally develop our brains for positive, successful, and rewarding relationships in life.

The three core capacities around which this handbook is based and organized by the following:

SELF-REFLECTION

Self-reflection is the ability to notice and name our experiences, including our feelings, thoughts, wants, intentions, and body sensations. As used in this handbook, it is the ability to observe our thoughts, feelings, and behavior in the moment as we participate in life. This capacity is often referred to as the "observing self" or the "silent watcher" that reflects on our thoughts and actions. Having the ability to notice and name our experience, to differentiate our experience from that of others, and to reflect on and learn from that experience is the foundation of emotional intelligence. It is the very driver of our capacity to learn and grow. This capacity can expand throughout our lifetimes, allowing us to enhance our ability to remain differentiated and aware in the midst of chaos and conflict. Self-awareness is the bedrock on which the other capacities are built.

EMPATHY

Empathy or compassion is the capacity to feel connected with another person and experience their pain or joy. It is the ability to "walk in another's shoes" and to understand what a given situation must feel like from their perspective. Individuals with highly developed empathy have the ability to stay connected to other people even during times of conflict, while individuals with underdeveloped empathy tend to emotionally disconnect from others during stressful times so as not to have to feel their own or another's pain. Empathic acknowledgment is the ability to interact with another person in ways that acknowledge, inquire about, and honor that person's experience, even when it is quite different from our own. It demands that we are able to maintain a level of self-differentiation even as we inquire about and truly listen to another's experience so as to avoid or repair ruptured relationships.

SELF-REGULATION

Self-regulation is the capacity to experience the distress and pain that are natural parts of life and to manage them in ways that help us reestablish our equilibrium or balance without requiring others to change. Individuals with highly developed emotional intelligence have a multitude of strategies for regulating their own emotions and their relationships in ways that do no harm, to themselves or others. A strong indication of healthy self-regulation is the ability to take responsibility for our own experience and choices even in the midst of stress. Healthy self-regulation accepts the world as it is, the joy and the sorrow, and moves toward taking self-responsibility in the moment. Well-developed self-regulation or self-soothing expands one's tolerance and ability to quickly recover in difficult situations.

The following chapters offer practices that are intended to help you increase your EQ fitness by developing these three core capacities. As you adopt these practices in your day-to-day life, you will also expand a number of related EQ competencies, both intrapersonal and interpersonal. Such internal or intrapersonal competencies include accurate self-assessment, trustworthiness, creativity, adaptability, commitment, initiative, resiliance and optimism. These external or interpersonal competencies include effective communication, conflict management, leadership, mentoring, social awareness, and cultural inclusiveness. When we have developed a greater awareness of ourselves and of others and can explore and tolerate differences among us, our expanded Emotional Intelligence allows us to live in relationship in ways that are personally and professionally rewarding and which powerfully contribute to our success in living.

Emotional Intelligence in the Workplace

With today's workplace demands, why bother with the development of Emotional Intelligence?

Does it make a REAL financial difference?

Does it make a REAL difference in leadership effectiveness?

Does it make a REAL difference in individual and organizational long-term success?

Organizations throughout the Western world have focused their efforts on obtaining the technical expertise to create and manage products and services, to be strategic, to take action, and to win. This focus has emphasized the "hard" skills required for success rather than the "soft" emotional and interpersonal skills of the people who make it all happen. But we now know that Emotional Intelligence makes a critical difference in individual and organizational success, a difference that people in the workplace can no longer ignore and that can lead to radical transformation. Research has shown us that with knowledge, awareness, and disciplined practice, we can literally modify our brains to build Emotional Intelligence and its gifts.

THE IMPACT OF EMOTIONAL INTELLIGENCE ON WORKPLACE PERFORMANCE

Daniel Goleman, in his book Working with Emotional Intelligence, provided the first widely researched data on the impact of Emotional Intelligence on performance in the workplace. Goleman's research was completed in collaboration with Hays/McBer, who provided extensive performance data collected from corporations world-wide and over many years.

The purpose of Goleman's research was to identify the key factors that supported high performance in the workplace across countries, continents, job functions, organizational size, and types of organizations. His findings are startling:

- Emotional Intelligence mattered twice as much as technical expertise or IQ.

- EQ accounted for 67% of the abilities deemed necessary for superior performance.

- At the highest level of complexity, Emotional Intelligence provided the only measurable advantage.

Research on the impact of emotional intelligence has continued in multiple quarters. In 2002, Cary Cherniss summarized the findings of a host of published studies about the impact of EQ in the workplace, which include the following:

- Deaths in intensive care units have been found to be four times greater when the nursing staff is depressed and emotionally unavailable to patients (Goleman, 2002).

- Insurance sales agents who were weak in such emotional competencies as self-confidence, initiative, and empathy sold policies with an average premium of just one-half the value of those of agents who were very strong in at least five of eight key emotional competencies (Hay/McBer Research and Innovation Group, 1997).

- In a large beverage firm, executives who were selected based on their strong emotional competence were far more likely to perform in the top third as measured by performance bonuses, accounting for 87% of the top third (McClelland, 1999).

- The primary causes of derailment in executive careers involved deficits in emotional competence, primarily (1) difficulty in handling change, (2) not being able to work well in a team, and (3) poor interpersonal relations (Center for Creative Leadership, 2007).

- New salesmen at Met Life who scored high on a test of "learned optimism" sold 37% more life insurance in their first two years than did pessimists (Seligman, 1990).

- A study of 130 executives found that how well people handled their own emotions determined how much people around them preferred to deal with them (Walter V. Clarke Associates, 1997).

TYPICAL LEADERSHIP BEHAVIORS OF LEADERS WITH STRONG OR WEAK EMOTIONAL INTELLIGENCE

Because Emotional Intelligence is always developed in relationship, from birth to death, better understanding how we manage ourselves in relationships can help us continue to develop our emotional competencies and lead to transformational change. To do this (as will be discussed later) requires attention to our relationships, awareness, intention, attention, and critical choices.

We all know that how leaders work with others is a critical factor in sustained high performance. In Social Intelligence and his other works, Goleman clearly articulates the impact leaders have on their organization and their direct reports. As he points out, our behavior is affected by our emotions whether we are conscious of them or not. Thus leaders who have highly developed self-awareness, self-regulation, and emotional capacity have the necessary foundation for the critical behaviors needed for success.

As part of his research, Goleman asked a wide range of people, from CEOs to schoolteachers, in cities throughout the Americas to describe what makes a good or bad boss. His results showed that "the best bosses are people who are trustworthy, empathic, and connected, who make us feel calm, appreciated, and inspired. The worst bosses—distant, difficult, and arrogant, who make us feel uneasy at best and resentful at worst" (Social Intelligence, 277).

Goleman's respondents' descriptions of Good Boss and Bad Boss behaviors were essentially the same across a myriad of different workplaces and roles, and included the following:

Good Boss	Bad Boss
Great Listener	Blank Wall
Encourager	Doubter
Communicator	Secretive
Courageous	Intimidating
Sense of Humor	Bad Temper
Shows Empathy	Self-Centered
Decisive	Indecisive
Humble	Arrogant
Shares Authority	Mistrusts

Emotional Intelligence is particularly critical for leaders because of the impact they have on every facet of organizational life, on others they work with, and on the continual and growing challenges they face daily. To be effective, leaders must both manage their own sense of emotional security and play a key role in creating a sense of security and safety for others.

One challenge that leaders (like all humans) often face is a gap between their own and others' perceptions of them. Leaders' awareness into the impact they have on others is often hampered because they do not get the "real news" from those around them. Leaders may believe they are humble when

others experience them as arrogant or believe they are good communicators when others perceive them as secretive and uncommunicative. Thus having the courage to directly ask others about one's impact on them can be a powerful step in identifying specific areas for powerful, focused leadership development.

To get a clear picture of what highly developed and underdeveloped emotional intelligence looks like in the workplace, common behaviors of each are listed below. These leadership behaviors often show up in 360 feedback surveys, feedback from bosses or board members, and/or feedback from customers. Overall, leaders with highly developed emotional intelligence can tolerate and even welcome information that will be helpful for their own learning or improvement within their organizational responsibility, while leaders with underdeveloped emotional intelligence tend to resist difficult information and become reactive as a way of protecting their emotional safety.

Leaders with Strong Emotional Intelligence:

- Observe themselves in the midst of the fray of business; they can identify what is happening with themselves and others and make informed choices in the midst of chaos.

- Lead with openness, honesty, and directness; genuinely invite others to do the same, and then listen carefully as others respond.

- Can change direction mid-course because they can continually observe themselves in mid-flight.

- Are aware of their impact on others.

- Bring a positive attitude that motivates others while maintaining an awareness of real problems or obstacles the team or organization faces.

- Use internal and external information and remain non-reactive in difficult situations.

- Listen to others, even when challenged.

- Appreciate differences and challenge others to explore, create, and be willing to make mistakes.

- Learn from their mistakes.

- Have a high degree of tolerance that allows for flexibility and resilience.

- Stay connected with others, even in the midst of conflict or stress.

- Are sensitive and appreciative of others while setting clear boundaries and maintaining accountability.

- Are aware of others with a high degree of accuracy, thus minimizing misinterpretations of others.

- Take the initiative to contact and hear from others during times of conflict and stress.

- Acknowledge others in positive, genuine, and understanding ways.

Leaders with Weak Emotional Intelligence:

- Have difficulty learning from their experience, particularly during conflict and when they feel at risk, and thereby repeat unproductive patterns of behavior again and again.

- Get angry, blame others, and stop listening.

- Have difficulty accepting bad news, leading others to censor the information they provide which results in leader's becoming isolated.

- Are often reactionary, with behavior ranging from withdrawal to volatile anger.

- Have difficulty understanding that they choose their response to a given situation.

- Have difficulty engaging others effectively in problem solving and making critical decisions.

- Withdraw or disconnect from others when challenged.

- Affect others in a way that leaves them feeling undervalued, dismissed, and/or not heard.

- Seek input from others to gain power and advantage rather than valuing other perspectives.

- Often focus on "winning" with limited regard to its impact on others.

The good news in all these findings is that leaders are made, not born, and the emotional intelligence and skills that make a leader effective can be learned and developed. The following chapters discuss practices that can be used to help improve any leader's emotional intelligence in the workplace.

Self-Reflection
Building Self-Awareness
and Choice

Choice begins the moment you become present. . . .

The mind, conditioned as it is by the past, always seeks to re-create what it knows and is familiar with. Even if it is painful, at least it is familiar. The mind always adheres to the known.

Present-moment awareness creates a gap not only in the stream of mind but also in the past-future continuum.

Nothing truly new and creative can come into this world except through that gap that clears the space for infinite possibility.

– Eckhard Tolle, *The Power of Now*

The first of the core competencies in EQ is the capacity for self-reflection, which we begin to develop in the first months of life. It starts as we gradually gain awareness that we are separate human beings: separate from others with our own intentions, thoughts, wants, and feelings. This ability to see ourselves as separate is the cornerstone for our learning to take responsibility for our own experiences and choices in day-to-day relationships.

Being conscious of these choices comes to us only when we are aware of our own experience in the moment and take responsibility for our experience and our interpretation of a given situation. Noticing our thoughts, wants, feelings, and our bodies in any given moment is the foundation for awareness and informed choice.

Following are nine specific practices that you can cultivate to develop self-awareness and choice.

Practice 1: Practice being present – stop to notice Now!

Stop several times a day to be fully present with yourself and the world around you. Notice your thoughts, wants, and feelings at those moments. Notice the sounds, smells, and bodily sensations of the world around you.

Notice:

- If you are inside, the room you are in and the objects around you.

- If you are outside, the human and natural world around you.

- The level and source of light.

- The air you are breathing. Is it fresh? Moving? Stale?

- The level of warmth or chill. Are you comfortable? Too chilly? Too warm?

- The sounds around you. What do you hear?

- The smells around you. What is their source? Are they pleasing? Unpleasant?

- The colors around you and how they feel to you. Are they bold and bright? Gray or dull?

- The texture and density of whatever is touching your body. Are your clothes comfortable? Uncomfortable?

Notice the above without judgment, just seeing and feeling the world around you. This will become easier with practice and typically will increase your sense of being grounded and having greater energy.

Practice 2: Notice your body—reduce "internal chatter" and stay present

To stay present in everyday life, it helps to be deeply rooted within yourself; otherwise, the mind, which has incredible momentum, will drag you along like a wild river.

It means inhabit your body fully. . . . To always have some of your attention in the inner energy field of your body. To feel your body from within, so to speak. It anchors you in the NOW."

Eckhart Tolle, *Practicing the Power of Now*

Everyone has experienced the difference between feeling fragmented and feeling solid and grounded. Being aware of our body often gives us an immediate sense of being more stable and in control of our energy. When we feel more grounded, we feel more confident and stable. Using one's body in this way can be a powerful stabilizer.

Practice:

- Feeling your feet, legs, arms, hands, your abdomen, and up through your head.

- Being still and feeling the quiet energy vibrating throughout your body, like a gentle pulsating glow. Can you feel the vibration and aliveness in your body?

- Noticing your entire body and staying there for as long as you feel comfortable.

- Taking five deep breaths and focusing on the quality and depth of your breathing. Try to clear your mind of all thoughts. This is a powerful method for getting out of one's head, stopping the endless "mind chatter," and becoming present. Invariably, this helps us experience increased focus and energy.

Practice 3: Practice naming and reflecting upon your experience

Practice becoming aware of your feelings:

Feelings are the ultimate driver of everything we do. Feelings are the part of our experience that defines the meaning of any given event and how important it is to us. Our interpretation of any event is first orchestrated by our feelings, which is only then followed by our analysis and understanding of an event and movement toward action. In other words, feelings "drive the bus." The key is whether we are aware of our feelings or not. When we lack awareness of our emotions, our actions are largely unconscious and place us at greater risk. When our fear is high, for example, it can obstruct clear thinking and move us to action prematurely. While that action may feel good at the moment, our satisfaction may unravel later when we realize we did not take time to gather all the information needed to make a wise choice.

Notice, name, and record the emotions you are feeling now. Do this regularly throughout the day to maintain your level of awareness in the moment. You can also do this at the close of the day, reflecting on what feelings you experienced over the course of the day. You may want to refer to the list of feelings included in the following chapter to help you remember or gain clarity about your emotions. Do this without judgment. The goal is just to notice and name.

Feelings add richness to our lives and expand our experience. Notice the nuances of your feelings and the feelings that lie under other feelings. Unbundling our feelings or "peeling the onion" around them can bring us clarity about what is really going on within us.

Practice becoming aware of your thoughts:

Watch your thoughts and judgments about yourself and others. Notice how your thoughts come and go without getting engaged in them. Notice what you are thinking without building on a thought by telling yourself a story. Just watch them come and go without judgment. When we are distressed, it is easy to hold on to a negative thought about another or a situation by building a story that supports that thought.

Practice becoming aware of your wants:

Practice starting your day by stating out loud to yourself or others one or more wants you have for this day: "Today I want . . . ." You might also state these wants in the form of an intention: "Today my intention is . . . " or "Today my commitment is. . . ." As you state out loud what you want from this day, notice your emotions and how they feel in your body. Stating your wants brings clarity and focused energy to guide you through your day.

Practice 4: Notice your level of intensity throughout the day

The foundation of emotional processing is the appraisal and arousal system, which can respond with various degrees of intensity . . . and the brain appears to be able to modify the intensity of the response.

Degrees of arousal have a wide range. The body's state of arousal is mediated by the brain. . . . The brain in turn monitors the state of the body and incorporates emotional meaning.

It is often at the moments in which emotion becomes most intense that we seem to have the greatest need to be understood and the most intense feelings of vulnerability. . . . At a moment of intensity, a failure to be understood and to not be connected with emotionally, can result in a profound feeling of shame . . . and can lead to withdrawal. Even with less intense states, not being understood may lead to a sense of isolation.

Daniel J. Siegel, *The Developing Mind*

Regardless of our individual day-to-day baseline level of intensity, emotionally charged situations increase our level of intensity and emotional vulnerability in the moment. The level of our emotional intensity in a given situation is often an indicator of the degree that our experience is being driven by past experiences.

Become aware of:

- Your base level of intensity. Would you or others call you an intense person? A low-key one?

- Whether you tend to express your level of intensity so that other people experience it directly or tend to mask or hold your intensity level inside yourself.

- When you are experiencing high intensity levels:

  - Think about how they may have interfered with your relationships at times.

- Notice how they affect your voice and your body.

- Stop talking and take several deep breaths, focusing on your breathing.

- Practice leaving the room and going outside to get fresh air or take a walk.

- When you are experiencing low intensity levels:

  - Think about how being "very laid back" may have interfered with your relationships at times.

  - Ask whether being detached sometimes keeps you from being fully engaged in living.

  - Practice speaking up and letting others know what you think, want, feel, and need. (Others may be misinterpreting your low intensity as a lack of caring.)

  - As a leader, state your intentions and wants clearly so others will not be left waiting to hear from you.

Practice 5: Focus on what you want, not on what you don't want

Many of us find it much easier to be clear about what we don't want than about what we do want. This is particularly true for those of us who have learned to focus on others, on making sure they get what they need or want, rather than attending to our own experience.

Practice identifying what you want by noticing each time that you find yourself focusing on what you do not want. Ask yourself, "What is my need that is not being met?" Make a note of that need and then move to identify some actions you can take to get it met.

Becoming aware of our human needs and finding ways to have them met enhances our life, vitality, and productivity by spending our energy on moving forward rather than resisting. Focusing our energies on what we don't like or want just drains us of precious energy.

Practice 6: Commit to journaling for one full month to increase self-awareness and choice

Writing our thoughts in a journal is an effective method for gaining self-awareness and noticing how we interpret our world and the people and situations we face each day. This is a practice that can be particularly valuable for individuals who tend to focus outside of themselves without stopping to notice and name their own experience.

The key to effective journaling is to focus on your own experiences and how you frame those experiences in your thoughts. This process can take many forms. You can write in a dedicated journal or writing pad or you can write notes to yourself on your computer. The key is to write about your own experience on a regular basis to heighten your awareness. This is your private journal, for your eyes only. You will learn about yourself by being totally honest and uncensored in your journaling.

One practice to heighten your awareness is to revisit your daily journal at the end of each week and circle all the feeling words that describe your own emotional responses to things. Do not circle feeling words you used to describe other peoples' feelings. Then ask yourself the following questions:

- Are feelings an integral part of how you experience your life?

- Does the emotional tenor of your writing tend to be positive or negative?

- Do you tend to focus your attention on yourself or on others?

- Do you tend to concentrate on actions you have taken or plan to take?

Highlight those thoughts, phrases, and expressions that make you feel light, warm, and powerful. Notice those moments and the difference they make for you.

The goal of this practice is to notice and gain awareness about how you experience yourself on a day-to-day basis. By the end of the month, it will be easy to see your patterns of thinking, wanting, feeling, and how positive or negative you tend to be on a daily basis.

Practice 7: Practice awareness of the stories you tell yourself

As life happens, we interpret it and give it meaning. We must do this to determine our responses and to function in our lives. Over a lifetime of experiences, each of us develops a deeply rooted internal map of how we view the world and ourselves in it.

This map is the basis of the stories we tell ourselves about ourselves, our lives, and the people around us. How we react and interact in any moment reflects the stories we have created out of our past experiences with our family, community, traditions, culture, and more. Their origins may even be centuries old, coming from a very long and powerful cultural tradition.

Without becoming aware of the stories we create to interpret our lives and direct our actions, and by so doing to also make space to create new ones, we are destined to continually repeat and recreate the past.

Practicing awareness of your own stories begins with:

- Understanding that they are your stories and only yours. You are the writer and editor of your own stories, which are unique to you. Remember that others' stories about the same situation may be very different than your own.

- Be responsible for your own story. Be aware of your story about the situation, about the other, about yourself in relationship with the other, and about your past that you are overlaying onto this moment.

- Knowing that you are free to create something new only when you become fully present and accept that your story is not the whole truth. Your story may be a powerful determinant of your success.

To build awareness of your own stories, commit to doing story journaling on a weekly basis. This process of journaling will heighten your awareness of the degree to which your stories focus on yourself or others and of how past experiences affect your responses in the present, especially during times of stress. Separating our past from the present is an essential process for heightening emotional intelligence. To do story journaling, select a situation that involves some emotional intensity (positive or negative) that you find yourself coming back to again and again. Then follow the steps below:

Step 1: Write a description of the situation and the other person.

- What happened?

- What did the other person say and do?

- What was the other person thinking, wanting, and feeling?

Step 2: Write a description of yourself in the situation. Write only about you.

- What did you want, think, and feel? What did you say? What was the impact of the situation on you?

- How is this situation living in you now?

Step 3: Reflect on if and how this experience is familiar to you.

- Have you experienced yourself and others in past situations in a similar way? Maybe it was years ago. Does your experience of yourself and the other fit with any childhood experiences that you remember?

- Reflect on the question above and then write what you remember about an experience from your past. Writing it out helps get clarity in seeing similarities.

Step 4: Identify any insights that have come to you and what it is that you want now.

- Write one specific action you are committed to taking. (One option is to do nothing.)

- Include a time frame for each action on your list.

Adapted from: Ron Short's *Stories*

Practice 8: Notice other people as mirrors of yourself

Scientists have recently discovered that we have "mirror neurons" in our brains, which are currently the subject of much research to understand the power of these neurons and their function in our daily relationships. Understanding how mirroring works can increase our ability to discover insights into our own experience through noticing others. According to Daniel Goleman's Social Intelligence,

Mirror neurons . . . reflect back an action we observe in someone else, making us mimic that action or have the impulse to do so. These do-as-she-does neurons offer a brain mechanism that explains the old lyric, "When you're smiling, the whole world smiles with you."

The human brain harbors multiple mirror neuron systems not just for mimicking actions but also for reading intentions, for extracting the social implications from what someone does, and for reading emotions.

Social skills depend on mirror neurons.

Our experience, our attitudes, and our feelings are contagious, as we are continuously reflecting each other or mirroring back the other person's experience. To become aware of how this mirroring affects our emotions and actions:

- Practice noticing others as mirrors of yourself.

- Notice positive and negative expressions of others' feelings and thoughts. How do these reflect or mirror you?

- Decide how you want to interact with others for one day or one week and intentionally practice it. For example, you might choose to acknowledge everyone you meet with a smile and a comment. Notice the response you get and the degree to which others mirror you in return. Try different responses to individuals and notice their response and then the impact their response has on you.

Practice 9: Join a group whose goal is to help one another practice awareness and choice

Most communities have a wide array of groups available that can help you explore how practicing greater awareness and choice can improve your life. These might include a variety of Twelve Step programs, focused learning groups, or meditation or spiritual development groups. If you don't have access to such a group, you could put one together of friends and colleagues who share your interest in gaining self-awareness and building positive relationships. What you will want to find is a group that supports:

- Self-awareness with self-discovery and self-responsibility.

- Acceptance and learning from a range of perceptions and attitudes. This will expand your level of tolerance, your flexibility, and your resilience.

- Trying out new behaviors that may initially feel risky but add richness and valuable skills for living.

- Being fully present and real in the moment, honoring yourself and others.

Self-Reflection –
Accessing a Wide Range
of Feelings

Knowing, feeling, and expressing all your emotions—
whether of love and joy or fear and anger—is good for your health.
It keeps you moving steadily though life. In fact, the word "emotion"
derives from a Latin verb meaning "to move" or "move out."
This is what our emotions do. They move us in the direction
in which we need to go in life. . . .
When you're able to identify, feel, and say, "I feel sad" or
"I feel angry" or "I feel grief" or "I feel fear," you can make the
appropriate moves, changes, and decisions that will enable you to
experience and enjoy your life to the fullest.

Mona Lisa Schulz, *Awakening Intuition*

Much has been studied and written about the role of emotion in our lives. Our feelings are the ultimate drivers of everything we do. We are either conscious of these drivers or not. Nonetheless, our feelings are in charge. In A General Theory of Love, the authors succinctly describe the limbic brain as being the "center of advanced emotionality" that actually takes in sensory data, determines the importance and meaning of the data, settles on an emotion, and then sends directions to the neocortical brain and the reptilian brain on how to respond. It is through this physiological process that our emotions are the ultimate drivers of everything we do.

We think of all feelings as being "essential," whether they feel good or are distressing. Each gives us valuable information on how our life is working. Being able to notice and name a broad spectrum of feelings can provide us with a depth of information that contributes to wisdom as well as richness and balance to our life experience. As John Bradshaw states in Healing the Shame That Binds You, "Our feelings are the primary motivating source in our lives. Without acknowledging our core feeling, we lose our sense of self."

Each significant feeling brings a gift of awareness as an important message to attend to. Some of these feelings and their associated gifts are listed here.

FEELING	THE GIFT IT BRINGS
Anger	Direction, motivation, and boundary setting
Anxiety	Clarity
Fear	Protection against harm
Joy	Emotional vitality—zest for living and involvement in life
Love	Warmth, caring for others
Sadness	Sensitivity to others' loss as well as one's own
Shame	Humility—knowing that as human beings we have limits and are "perfectly imperfect"

This section provides practices for each of the major feeling groups that are measured in the EQ in Action Profile. Each feeling bears a gift and has implications if we under- or over-rely on it.

Practices to Increase Access to Your Feelings and Manage Your Moods

All feelings can be both a blessing and a curse, depending upon the degree we experience them and the degree they tend to take over our entire experience when we are challenged. Although feelings bring us important messages, dwelling on a particular distressful feeling can cloud or distort our experience.

Practice 1: Notice your emotions as just passing moods rather than defining life events

Research has shown that individuals who have the ability to experience and name their feelings are more aware of their moods and far less affected by them. The ability to identify and name feelings provides a more stable interpretation of oneself and life around us.

- At the end of each day, use a chart such as the following chart practice noticing your predominant mood for the day.

- Rate your degree of satisfaction with your life each day on a scale of 1-10.

- At the close of the month, review your entries. What were your predominant moods? What caused any swings? Did this pattern change by devoting specific attention and awareness to it?

Adapted from Joseph Ciarrochi, Joe Forgas, and John D. Mayer,
Emotional Intelligence in Everyday Life

The Date	My Dominant Mood Today	My Satisfaction Rating	My Feelings Today Included
1)			
2)			
3)			
4)			
5)			
6)			
Etc.			

Practice 2: Identify what feelings you want more access to

Circle feelings or emotions you want to gain greater awareness of:

Anger	Anxiety	Fear	Joy	Love	Sadness	Shame
Agitated	Anxious	Alarmed	Alive	Attention	Crushed	Ashamed
Anger	Confused	Defensive	Bold	Caring	Disappointed	Burdened
Annoyed	Distant	Doubtful	Brave	Comforting	Discouraged	Condemned
Appalled	Dulled	Dread	Capable	Compassion	Distraught	Culpable
Disgusted	Frantic	Fearful	Comfortable	Concerned	Distressed	Despised
Frustrated	Helpless	Frightened	Confident	Encouraged	Empty	Disgraced
Irritated	Impatient	Reluctant	Curious	Engaged	Grief	Dread
Outraged	Intense	Startled	Delighted	Gentle	Lonely	Embarrassed
Rage	Nervous	Suspicious	Dynamic	Honored	Lost	Guilty
Spiteful	Overwhelmed	Tense	Eager	Open	Miserable	Harassed
Upset	Paralyzed	Worried	Elated	Respected	Mournful	Humiliated
Vindictive	Perplexed		Energized	Secure	Remorseful	Inept
	Queasy		Excited	Tender	Resigned	Inadequate
	Skeptical		Glad		Sad	Regretful
	Stressed		Gleeful		Sorry	Shame
	Uneasy		Hopeful		Terrible	
			Joyful			
			Optimistic			
			Passionate			
			Peaceful			
			Relaxed			
			Safe			
			Self-assured			
			Surprised			

Practice attending to the possibility of these feelings showing up for you. When they show up, even if only slightly and briefly, note what triggered the feeling and how it felt in your body. Our bodies can be powerful in helping us clearly experience a feeling. Express appreciation to yourself for this new feeling. Say "way to go" to yourself. Once we feel a given emotion, it gets easier to notice and understand. Notice the situation or context in which you felt this emotion. Is there something to learn from this?

Practice 3: Practice "unbundling" your feelings

When our feelings are intense, we often bundle several of them together into one predominant feeling. The practice of sorting out all of our feelings adds richness to our life experience and provides valuable information that can free us from the intensity of the past. It also helps us make informed decisions now. Think of it as peeling the layers of an onion, noticing whether other feelings are hidden below the prevailing feeling.

If you often feel irritation or anger, for instance, notice what feelings lie beneath the anger and the origin of those feelings. If you feel anxious or sad, practice identifying and naming the underlying emotions. Shame, for example, may be a form of anger aimed at yourself, and sometimes sadness contains elements of shame because of the helplessness you may feel.

Practice 4: Practice identifying your feelings several times a day

Remember that our feelings drive everything we do. As I often put it, our emotions "drive the bus," whether or not we are aware of it. Having easy, rapid access to a wide range of feelings puts us in charge. Whether or not we express those feelings is another choice. We always benefit from simply noticing and naming them.

Practice the following when you wake up, at work, in meetings, with family members or friends and as you fall asleep at night.

- Notice patterns in different contexts in your daily life.

- Notice what triggers certain emotions. (For example, what happened just prior to your feeling irritated?) Make a list of these triggers to identify patterns.

- Ask others close to you how they experience you and your feelings. Some people find it easier to identify an emotion when another names it for them.

- If you are in an intense situation and are unable to identify what you feel, notice your body. Is it tense, is your jaw or shoulders tight, do you feel slumped over? Focusing on that part of your body can be a powerful portal for identifying the feeling that is affecting your body.

Practice to Experience and Manage Your Unrecognized Anger

Many of us have unacknowledged anger that can affect our performance and relationships. To become more familiar with such unrecognized anger, practice noticing when:

- You maybe feeling disappointed, hurt, or sad. These feelings may indicate some anger that you are not feeling directly.

- You do not feel anger during a difficult moment but may later feel like you have been taken advantage of.

- Your spouse or friends get angry when they hear some of your stories and yet you do not feel that anger yourself.

- You find it difficult to set your boundaries and say no.

- You are feeling fatigue from overstretching yourself with commitments.

Each of the above may indicate anger that you are not giving yourself permission to feel. The gift of anger is motivation, direction, and setting boundaries. It helps us know when we are being violated in some way by others. When you have any of the experiences noted above or experience something similar, practice the following:

- Notice your body. Is it relaxed or tense? (Our bodies can be excellent indicators of what is going on with us emotionally.)

- Giving yourself permission to feel irritated, frustrated, or angry. Tell yourself it is okay.

- Noticing if allowing yourself to feel anger creates anxiety for you in some way. There is a reason you are not allowing yourself to feel angry, whether it is guilt, fear, or something else. Try to notice what messages you tell yourself that make it difficult for you to feel anger and honor that for yourself. Write anything that comes to mind.

- Feeling angry without expressing it. Giving yourself the freedom to notice the anger and experience it without needing to express it makes it safe for you to practice noticing your anger.

- Noticing the other feelings listed above and any other distressing feelings to learn if anger is underneath. When you notice anger, ask yourself what you want. (You do not need to share this. However, it will help you get clarity by using all aspects of your experience.)

Practices to Experience and Manage Your Conscious Anger

Anger is one of our earliest feelings and thus the neural pathways it travels in our brains are deep and wide. To manage intense anger requires noticing and naming it in the moment, without making judgments about it. Understanding what triggers our anger and then noticing it in the moment is the key to managing anger in any aspect of our lives.

Anger can be suppressed, expressed in unhealthy ways, or expressed in healthy ways. Suppressed anger is still felt and can easily contribute to chronic physical disease. Understanding our anger and learning ways to express it without hurting ourselves or others is essential for healthy relationships.

In *Taking Charge of Anger*, Robert Nay examines what he terms the "faces of anger" and provides a checklist to identify when anger is a problem. Some of the items on this checklist include the following:

- Does my anger negatively affect others?
- Is my health or quality of life suffering because of my anger?
- Is anger affecting my efficiency and performance?
- How intense is my anger and how long does it last?

Below is a partial list of ways in which anger manifests itself. Notice the degree to which you identify with any of them.

Suppression of Anger	Openly Aggressive Anger	Passive-Aggressive Anger
o Withdrawal from problems o Refusing to expose personal problems o Being image-conscious, wanting to appear totally together o Letting frustration pass without saying anything o Being a people pleaser o Refusing to let others help o Pretending to not be resentful o Succumbing to others and resenting it	o Loud communication that does not allow room for others' ideas o Being blunt and opinionated o Bickering, complaining, griping o Insulting speech with cursing o Generally pessimistic o Insisting on having the last word o Giving unwanted advice o Reactivity and rebutting others	o Being silent when you know what the other person wants of you o Procrastinating and chronic forgetfulness o Doing things as you want them even when you know it disrupts others o Being evasive o Repeatedly saying, "I don't know" o Putting off responsibility o Giving half-hearted effort

Adapted from Les Carter, *The Anger Trap*

The first step in understanding and managing anger is to look deeply and honestly inside yourself to identify how you experience anger and how you express it. Following are four practices that can help you do this.

Practice 1: Heighten your awareness of and your ability to manage anger

When your anger is "triggered," focus inside your body and take six slow deep belly breaths before responding.

Focus inside rather than on the other. Take responsibility for your own feelings to avoid blaming others. Just notice your level of anger, from mild irritation to rage.

Notice the hurt or other feelings beneath your anger. Suspend any response; just notice your anger until you identify the underlying feelings. This practice will help dissipate your anger and give you added information for use in your response.

Practice 2: Notice your "self-talk" or "automatic thoughts" that create and sustain angry moods

The authors of A General Theory of Love describe a mood as "a state of enhanced readiness to experience a certain emotion." A mood can be created and extended by thoughts about a given emotion. So when one feels a degree of anger, this can be expanded into a mood by repetitive thinking about the anger and the story one creates about the event that triggered the anger. Given that the gradual decrease in neural activation in our brain takes several minutes, it easy to provoke anger again and again within this window, turning a feeling of anger into a mood.

Our core brain physiology makes us susceptible to creating and sustaining moods of anger, which is supported by our self-talk or self-chatter. The internal self-chatter of individuals who get caught in angry moods will be dominated by negative thoughts about the situation or the other. There are two helpful options for intervening in this process:

1. Stop the self-talk that is consistent with the anger. Saying STOP out loud is useful and effective in interrupting the pattern. This practice may require saying STOP again and again while the neural activity diminishes and we realize we have choices in the moment.

2. State your self-talk to yourself out loud. This process engages the neocortex in a way that can allow you to notice what is accurate or true and what is not. This is very effective and helps us become current rather than getting caught in the automatic, predicable self-talk that reinforces anger.

Practice 3: Anger intervention begins with self-awareness and choice

The following are ways to use self-awareness and choice to gain control over anger:

- Prevention: Say "no" to the small stuff.

- Notice how your body is giving you cues about your growing anger.

- Recognize you control your anger and can choose your response.

- Use anger "down" talk vs. anger "up" talk, such as the following:

   This is not a big deal. I can let it go.

   - I need to think before I speak.

   - I can stay calm in this moment.

   Adapted from Deborah Griffing, master class *in Working with Anger*

Practice 4: Self-instructions for the regulation of anger

A quick response when we are angry is typically a patterned response and can catch us by surprise when an incident occurs that replicates a past experience that also included anger. Anger is one of our earliest and strongest emotions and can easily arouse and be hijacked by the amygdala portion of our brain. It is useful to have a plan for regulation of anger and to practice response options that will help you be less reactive and stay in control. The following practice, adapted from Robert Nay's *Taking Charge of Anger*, is based upon the knowledge that although anger is powerful and we can be easily captured by it, we can also stay in control with sufficient preparation and practice.

The following are self-instructions or intentional self-talk that can be employed at different stages of experiences that trigger anger:

Preparation for Provocation

Write out some specific phrases, such as the following, that fit for you and practice using them so when you get in a provocative situation it is easy to access your practiced thoughts.

- This may upset me, but I know how to deal with it.

- I can work out a plan to handle this. My plan is to ___.

- Remember, stick to the issues and don't take it personally.

- I can take deep breaths to relax myself and to think more clearly.

- Easy does it, I am in control.

Impact and Confrontation

Select a simple method of relaxation, such as the following, and routinely practice it so it is easily available to you when your anger is triggered.

- Stay calm. Just continue to relax.

- As long as I keep my cool, then I'm in control of the situation.

- There is nothing to be gained by getting mad.

- What difference will this make in a week or a month?

- When I stay calm, I can think clearly.

Arousal of Anger

Prepare and practice self-messages, such as the following, that you can use to help you become aware of and to cope with the arousal of anger before taking action.

- My muscles are getting tight. That's my signal for a relaxation exercise.

- Time to take a deep breath and slowly image a positive outcome.

- Move into my problem-solving skills.

- Focus on behavior, not what she or he wants. Focus on the impact on me and own my reaction as my responsibility.

After Confrontation

After the situation is over, practice the following to deepen your self-understanding and effectiveness in dealing with anger.

- Reflect on how you handled the situation and think about anything about your response that may have been more effective. Write this out and put a practice in place to build your brain muscles.

- Reflect on what you did that worked for you, including the degree to which you relied on your relaxation and your anger management skills.

Practices to Manage Anxiety

The gift of healthy anxiety is awareness and clarity. In contrast, high anxiety often creates some feelings of disorientation that make it hard to focus and think clearly at the moment. High anxiety can be immobilizing. It can also create panic that results in impulsive, disorganized, and reactive actions. In Welcome to Your Crisis, Laura Day suggests that when you find yourself caught in a high level of anxiety, it can be helpful to "interrupt the process by shifting your focus to an activity. . . . This is not a time to think things through." Moving from thinking to engaging in a tactile project can be very helpful. This can be anything that takes your mind away from circular thinking. Cleaning the house or garage, washing the car, working in the garden, or any other task that engages your body can help move you out of your mind and into your body, which has its own quieting intelligence. The following practices will help you learn to identify the triggers that generate anxiety and move quickly to an appropriate response that you have practiced in advance.

Practice 1: Reduce anxiety by accepting it and letting it float past you like a cloud on a windy day

You can control your thoughts and your breathing but you can't control your adrenaline. Once adrenaline gets released into your bloodstream, you're going to feel anxious and uncomfortable for a few minutes. To get past anxiety, learn to accept this feeling rather than fight it.

When you can just watch your anxiety float by without listening to it, your adrenaline will quickly subside. With practice you can:

- Detach from feelings and just observe your bodily sensations and feelings.

- Stop listening to your accompanying thoughts. (Thinking negative judgments about yourself or the other will keep anxiety going and strengthen it.)

- Practice being an observer of yourself.

  Adapted from Matthew McKay, Martha Davis and Patrick Fanning,
  Thoughts and Feelings: Taking Control of Your Moods and Your Life

Practice 2: Heighten understanding of your anxiety and identify your unique triggers

Write a description of real situations that generate high anxiety for you.
Practice noticing when you are feeling anxious and identify what prompts it.
In your journal or business calendar, jot down a description of what preceded
the feeling of anxiety. Be as specific as you can to help identify particular
triggers. Note the degree of anxiety raised by the situation.

Describe the situation:

- Record the specific actions or interactions that spark or contribute to
  your anxiety.

- Record the thoughts that accompany your anxiety.

- Rate the degree of your anxiety (1=low, 10=high).

- Rate the degree to which your anxiety is based on today's reality
  versus past fear (1=today, 10=past).

- Note what you do next.

As you identify more of these triggering events and your responses to
them, examine what common denominators emerge.

Describe situation	Rank anxiety level (1-10)	Your thoughts	Reality ranking (1=based on today 10= based on past)	What you did next

Practice 3: Strengthen your ability to manage anxiety

Identify negative internal messages about yourself that trigger your anxiety. Then rewrite these messages and consistently use them as affirmations in a focused, deliberate manner. The neuroplasticity of our brain structure allows this disciplined practice to actually reorganize the brain's resources. Research has documented the ability to make radical changes in our brains by approaching a practice with focused attention and intention.

Using the following form as an example, write down the situation that triggered the anxiety and the negative internal messages it sparked for you. Rewrite these messages in a positive manner that you can use daily to reorganize the neural pathways in your brain. Transfer those positive messages to a card or form you can see regularly or carry with you to review them on a daily basis.

Step 1: Describe the situation
E.g., I have multiple things to accomplish in a short amount of time. I'm feeling anxious.

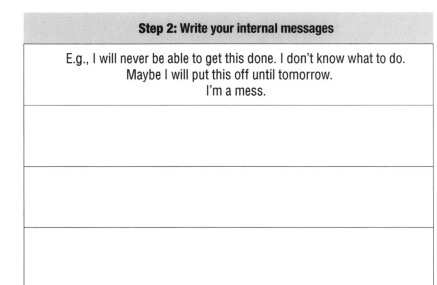

Step 2: Write your internal messages

E.g., I will never be able to get this done. I don't know what to do.
Maybe I will put this off until tomorrow.
I'm a mess.

Step 3: Rewrite each message to be positive

E.g., I can get this done by focusing on one thing at a time.
I can start now with the easiest task so I can check it off.
I am a capable human being.

Practice 4: Manage your anxiety in trigger situations

All of the following can help you manage anxiety in situations that tend to trigger it for you:

- When preparing for a project, presentation, or any upcoming anxiety-laden meeting or event, take time to plan as thoroughly as you can in advance. Write down the specific steps, processes, and timelines so if you "get lost," a frequent symptom of anxiety, you will have a reference point for getting back on track.

- Seek help from others in advance of a potentially difficult situation. When you can, partner with a colleague to work with you on projects or to just be aware and support you in potentially difficult situations.

- When you partner with someone on a project, presentation, facilitation, or coaching, think through what they can watch for and what kind of help you would like from them when your anxiety is heightened in non-productive ways.

Practices to Manage Fear

Fear, like all emotions or feelings, is an essential and primal part of being a human being. Its gift is protection and safety. Without a healthy level of fear, we would not live long. The keys to managing fear are, first, to be able to notice and name it; second, to determine whether the level of fear is congruent with the situation; and third, using that fear to move toward some action that will provide appropriate protection for the given situation. Trouble arises when fear is activated in a powerful way from the past.

Fear can be immobilizing or it can activate us to take charge in a way that helps us push through the fear that will expand our emotional capacity, enhance our resilience, give us the confidence to trust our ability to handle whatever life hands us, and allow us to experience our power rather than helplessness.

In one of my all-time favorite books, *Feel the Fear and Do it Anyway,* Susan Jeffers acknowledges that we all fear—it is a natural part of life. But, she argues, we can learn to manage it and use it in highly effective ways. As she puts it,

> *Fear seems to be epidemic in our society. We fear beginnings; we fear endings. We fear changing; we fear "staying stuck." We fear success; we fear failure. We fear living; we fear dying. . . . Whenever we take a chance and enter unfamiliar territory or put ourselves into the world in a new way, we experience fear. Very often this fear keeps us from moving ahead with our lives. The trick is to feel the fear and do it anyway.*

The following practices can help us identify the true cause of our fear and to work our way past it.

Practice 1: Steps to manage your fear

Identify situations that trigger your fear. What is the common denominator for you? How is your past heightening your fear now? Often intense fear is prompted not by actual danger but by past experiences. When both fear and shame are activated, the original fear is heightened by the added fear that you may be shamed or humiliated. To better understand your fears, write about the following in your journal:

- List the situations that trigger your fear.
- Notice how these situations elicit early life or other past experiences.
- Is there a pattern in your triggers?

When you notice a fear trigger being activated, practice moving quickly to repeating, "I am safe, I am safe, I am safe," which can interrupt your reactive pattern. Block yourself from thinking about your fear, as such thoughts tend to activate and maintain it. By stopping the thoughts and focusing on the mantra above, you should experience a significant diminishing of fear in a few minutes.

Partner with friends, family members, and/or colleagues regarding situations that generate fear for you. Ask them to listen carefully to you and others as these situations arise and be aware of their own experience. Friends and colleagues can help by minimizing any misinterpretation of what is happening now and providing support that can help you be fully present and overcome your fear.

Practice 2: Practice feeling more powerful in the face of your fear

To get beyond the helplessness that is often engendered by fear, try the following practices:

- In writing, list the payoffs you get from staying stuck in a situation, relationship, or some other aspect of your life. What does it keep you from having to so or face? What comfort do you get from it? What image do you get to hold on to? Be as honest with yourself as you can. Putting your responses in writing will help you name your fears and help you see possibilities.

- Be aware of all the options you have during the course of a given day. When you are confronted with a difficult situation, think about and write out all the ways you might act and feel about what just happened. This will help you to discover alternatives.

- Start noticing what you say in conversations with friends. Does it include complaining about other people?

- List the many choices available to you that can change upsetting situations into positive ones.

- Practice going one full week without criticizing anyone (including yourself) or complaining about anything. Notice your increased sense of control and power.

Adapted from Susan Jeffers, *Feel the Fear and Do It Anyway*

Practice 3: Manage your fear related to work, your performance, and your success

Set aside some quiet time at home and identify work situations, either past or anticipated, that generate fear for you. Using the grid below as an example, name the situation and the fear. Rate the intensity of the fear and the likelihood that this situation will ever actually occur. Notice the origin of this fear. When fear is intense, it most likely is related to an early life experience.

When you determine the fear is related to your past and most likely will not happen now, honor the fear and let it go. Then stop the associated thoughts. One effective option at these moments is to repeat to yourself, "I am safe now, I am safe now" as many times as necessary for the fear to diminish.

Lastly, identify an action you can take to gain more clarity about the source of your fear and/or to reduce your risk.

Name the situation that generates fear	Rate the intensity of your fear (1-10)	Name the worst thing that could happen

Rate the likelihood of that happening (1-10)	Identify the origin of this fear; honor it and let it go	Define an action you will take to gain clarity and reduce your risk

Practices to Increase Joy and Emotional Vitality

Complete Energy = Physical Energy + Emotional Energy

We now know that the physical energy side is actually the less important part. I asked energy experts such as endocrinologists, nutritionists, and specialists in sports medicine, "How much energy does the typical American get from physical sources and how much from emotional ones?" . . . I was stunned to learn that physical energy can supply at most 30% of your total energy. Even if you have perfect health, eat a good diet, and get the perfect amount of exercise, all that would give you only 30% of the complete energy you need. The remaining 70% of the energy you need must come from your emotional energy. And you need a lot.

Mira Kirshenbaum, *The Emotional Energy Factor*

Joy is the emotional energy that is the essential source of life. It provides us the emotional vitality and zest to engage in life. It is the fuel that gives us the energy to be open, to explore, to enjoy challenges, and to invite participation in the world around us. So individuals who enjoy a high degree of joy have the emotional energy to learn, to take risks, to quickly recover, and to enjoy the game of life.

So low joy is depletion of the very energy that is the source of our life. It may be experienced as fatigue, burnout, depression, or a general feeling of flatness or lack of energy for emotional involvement with life. One's feelings, body, and thoughts may lack brightness, clarity, and luster. We can feel the lack of emotional energy in our bodies.

It is not uncommon for a person to be extremely successful in their outer world and receive the financial and personal rewards of that success while at the same time being emotionally depleted. When this happens, we can be "running on empty" and doing what needs to be done without noticing the creeping emotional depletion until one day, as Kirshenbaum puts it, "it hits you that your emotional tires have gone flat."

Building and sustaining joy or emotional energy is essential to enjoy life at its fullest. Restoring joy in our lives begins with turning our focus back on ourselves rather than the world outside of us, no matter how much we may have achieved in the professional world. Often the loss of joy results from a lifetime of caring for or focusing on others at our own expense.

Following are four sets of practices that can help us refill the joy in our tanks.

Practice 1: Increase your joy, vitality, and energy for living

- Practice being present without judging yourself or others.

- Be silent and notice your body and the life energy that is flowing through it. Be present and rest within your body in silence. Allow a few minutes for this practice daily.

- Increase your physical exercise – do something you enjoy at least four times a week.

- Identify three things that bring you energy and joy, and build them into your daily routine.

- Post the above three things where you will see them often. Repeat them to yourself in your meditation or silent moments when you are in traffic or waiting anywhere.

- Focus on yourself with appreciation. Write three to five things you really appreciate about yourself. (This does not need to be shared with anyone but will bring you home to your own emotional energy.)

- Notice your nutrition. Reduce sugar and simple carbohydrates. Attend to your body and your own self-care, whatever that may be for you.

Practice 2: Practice defining what you want and doing it your way

It is important to notice what you want, not just what is needed or what you should do. Give yourself permission to define what you want, whether you act on it or not.

- As you wake in the morning, have your first cup of coffee, or take a morning walk, ask yourself, "What do I want today?" Give yourself permission to be honest. Put away any "shoulds" or internal thoughts that tell you your desire is impossible. We are not talking about taking action here, just genuinely asking yourself and listening to an honest response. This is honoring of yourself and will help you feel grounded for the day. Most likely you will feel heightened emotional energy in your body.

- Ask the question above every day for one week or one month. Write down your responses. Again, you do not need to tell anyone, and while you can take action for the day, that is not the requirement here. The purpose is to gain awareness of and access to your emotional energy and track it.

- On a weekly basis, look over your responses to "What do I want today?" Were they similar or different each day? Did you act on any of them? Is there a pattern to what you want? Prioritize your stated wants from highest priority to lowest.

- Make a commitment to act on your highest priority. This can be a baby step or a giant action. It is giving yourself permission and making space in your life for yourself. It will add emotional energy to your life.

When you make this commitment, large or small, over time you will feel an increase in your emotional energy, your overall vitality, and your increased availability for relationships that involve emotional energy.

Practice 3: Managing your depletion

- Notice when you are feeling depleted and used up. Go inside yourself and listen to what your body has to tell you. Listen to your breathing; notice the energy in your body. Stop and give yourself a break.

- Express appreciation to yourself and your need to recover your emotional energy. Be supportive of yourself. Avoid any judgments of yourself. If you find your internal chatter includes self-judgment, say STOP out loud and move your focus elsewhere. This negative internal chatter adds to your depletion.

- Commit a designated time to restore yourself daily and weekly. The focus here should be on what is nurturing to you and your soul, as opposed to doing something just for fun. Some methods that are effective for many people include:
  - Prayer.
  - Meditation.
  - Doing something new, anything that takes you out of your routine and is stimulating to you and your brain. Make sure this is something you enjoy doing.
  - Visualizing yourself filled with emotional energy and vitality. (Extensive research documents this can have dramatic effects for building our own emotional energy.)

- Make four lists of how you spend your time and energy in the world. In the first list, write all the things you do that bring you life energy and that you want to do. On the second list, list all the things that are "shoulds" or things you "need to do" for whatever reason but no longer add zest or energy to your life. On the third list, include things in your life that take life energy without any reciprocity, thereby contributing to your depletion. On the fourth list, select at least one thing from the third list, something that is contributing to your depletion, and replace it with at least one thing you will add to your daily life to increase your emotional energy.

Adapted from Mira Kirshenbaum, *The Emotional Energy Factor*

Practice 4: Practicing self-care

- Select one or more actions from the list below that you can adopt as part of your commitment to self-awareness and self-care:

- Leave a situation temporarily to get grounded and then return.

- Walk or exercise.

- Meditate or pray.

- Seek relationships that enrich you and bring you life.

- Notice your depletion without judgment.

- Listen to music, read, sing, play an instrument.

- Laugh.

- Participate in a sports or physical activity.

- Focus on what you want and act on it.

- Spend some time in nature.

- Add plants to your office or home (which has proven to be beneficial).

- Participate in a support group that focuses on awareness, self-care, and choice.

- Think of a time in your life that was simply joyful for you. What about that experience gave you joy and life? Define the essential nature of that experience that you can add to other life experiences.

- Take time for silence where you simply notice and feel the energy that supports your body and breathing. This will be grounding and add vitality. It is also a way of honoring and respecting yourself and your body that supports your life every moment.

Practices to Increase Positive Feelings toward Others

Having the ability to experience positive, caring feelings toward others is essential for creating and sustaining healthy relationships with others, both personally and professionally. Without positive feelings and concern for others, we are unable to remain connected to others in a way that supports life. When our positive feelings toward others are reduced, which is common when we are being challenged by those others, we tend to withdraw or pull away emotionally to protect ourselves. This is logical in many ways, but the consequences can be significant when this pulling away is extreme. The impact can be a loss of trust on the part of others and a response in kind. Empathy deteriorates and both parties tend to move toward protecting their own emotional energy, eroding the relationship, rather than moving closer to each other. When this pattern is overused, the capacity for intimacy may be eroded.

In A General Theory of Love, the authors note that "From birth to death, love is not just the focus of human experience but also the life force of the mind, determining our moods, stabilizing our bodily rhythms, and changing the structure of our brains. . . . Love makes us who we are and who we can become." The kind of love they are is referring to is much broader than "falling in love." Adult love depends upon knowing the other, mutuality between persons, and synchronous attunement between people. When love is missing, we tend to isolate ourselves from others, which places us at emotional and physiological risk. Without connection with others, our stability in the world is compromised.

The following are practices you can follow to increase your positive feelings toward others and avoid such isolation.

Practice 1: Notice when you begin pulling away or withdrawing your emotional energy from the other

We most typically tend to withdraw emotionally from another person when we have been challenged by that person or are in the midst of conflict with them. When you find this happening, can take the following steps.

Notice:

- Your thoughts—what are you thinking about the other?

- Your feelings that contribute to your pulling away.

- Your body's reaction to this conflict.

Practice:

- Relaxing your body.

  o Being as transparent as possible with the other person. Share something about your own reactions, and only about yours. For example, "I'm confused," "I'm hurt," "I need more information," "I need to think about this."

  This simple action will help you stay more connected to the other and decrease the likelihood they will pull away and reduce their trust in you.

  o Noticing something about the other person that is neutral or positive for you. Focus on this neutral or positive aspect for a moment to move toward an appreciation of and connection with the other.

Practice 2: Remember a relationship or interaction where you felt very loved and cared for and overlay this on your current situation

In **Train the Mind, Change Your Brain**, Sharon Begley notes the finding of an extensive research study conducted by Phillip Shaver and Mario Mikulincer in Israel and the United States that "having a sense of being loved and surrounded by supporting others seems to allow people to open themselves to alternative worldviews and be more accepting of people who do not belong to their own group. . . . It has something to do with love." This research shows the powerful effect on current difficult relationships of connecting with a part of us that has been loved and comforted in the past. The following are some practices that can help you make such connections.

- When you are approaching a difficult situation with someone you react negatively to or tend to pull away from, "prime" yourself for this interaction by getting quiet within and picturing an interaction with a person in your past or present with whom you feel safe and fully supported. Place yourself in that situation, noticing and enjoying that experience. Take time to experience this with your whole self, both your mind and your feelings, and notice the comfort it provides and how it lowers your anxiety or defensiveness.

- Immediately after the above step, enter a conversation or a meeting with the person that you anticipate will be difficult and may include conflict. Research shows that you will most likely be more open to the individual and be able to access positive feelings toward them, including having more compassion.

Practice 3: Practice seeing the face of someone you love and overlaying this face on a person you find difficult to care about

This practice is similar to the above and can also produce profound results. It requires that you intentionally move toward positive feelings for the other and that you pay attention to the process. The brain has a tremendous ability to change itself through neuroplasticity, but doing so requires rigorous attention. Honestly ask yourself if you really want to change how you experience this person (intention) and whether you are willing to make the effort to overlay the person's face with a face you love. If so, it can be a very effective way of opening yourself to be loving to a difficult or challenging person in your life.

Practice 4: Practice gratitude each day

Each morning or evening, take a few quiet minutes and state out loud and ideally write out four things you are grateful for this day. This exercise will help you become present and grounded and interrupt worry and negative thinking. It is useful to do this in your calendar, your journal, or in a work notebook that you keep so you can go back and look at it from time to time.

This can be a simple as "I'm grateful for the sun this day," "I'm grateful for spring," "I'm grateful for my health," or "I'm grateful for my comfortable bed." It is helpful to include tactile and sensory items, as they will help you get out of your head and negative thinking and just state something you are genuinely grateful for.

This practice can be linked with the "what I want this day" exercise as well, which can really start the day in a positive, empowered way.

Practices to Manage Sadness

*You have and will have sadness. It might be the
loss of a job, pet, or loved one. Yes, even a loved one.
The trouble is particularly here in the United States, we have
a quick-fix for everything . . . .why not sadness too?*

*Our quick-fix for sadness is that it's simply not allowed.
Healthy purging of sad feelings is great for you physically and
wonderful for your mental health. When you stuff the
expression of healthy sadness it may lead to health problems,
interpersonal issues and depression.*

*So, the first lesson is FEEL your sadness over whatever issue is
at hand. It doesn't make you weak or less a man or woman to do so.*

Dave Turo-Shields, *"How to Tell Sadness from Depression"*

Sadness is an essential feeling in life, one that every person experiences to
some degree and many to a level of devastation. While sadness is painful, it
can also bring sensitivity and compassion for ourselves and for others. It can
bring with it the gift of soulfulness and increased depth of being. Most of us
know someone who has lived through unimaginable pain, sadness, and grief
and emerged as a wise, loving being who has much grace to give to others.
Trying to escape sadness through drugs or repressing our feelings deprives
us of an important part of our life journey.

Accepting and feeling sadness is the first and critical step in healing loss,
which contributes to a revitalization of emotional energy and a renewed
involvement with life. Honoring a child's sadness over a loss, whether it is
perceived as critical or trivial by an adult, is essential for their healing and
their revitalization as well. Without living with and through loss, life may be
dulled as a person moves to protect oneself from the pain.

Because sadness is an acceptable feeling in our culture whereas anger and shame are not, it is not uncommon that other feelings are bundled or hidden under sadness. When your sadness is heightened, it is helpful to peel the onion of sadness to explore if other essential feelings are buried within it.

Practice 1: Notice your sadness and allow yourself to feel and express it

- Allow yourself to notice and name the feeling of sadness.

- Allow yourself to feel it in your body—it may feel heavy and even physically painful.

- First express your sadness to yourself. This is an important step in acknowledging and accepting your whole self.

- Express your sadness to others as seems appropriate to you and feels safe.

Practice 2: Explore whether feelings of anger or shame are hidden under your sadness

Anger and shame are essential feelings from which we can benefit only when we are conscious of them. Sadness has an element of hopelessness, of something that cannot be changed but simply lived with. In contrast, feeling appropriate anger can be boundary setting and can move us to protect ourselves or take appropriate action. The following can help you determine if your sadness is covering up legitimate feelings of anger or shame:

- Notice when others around you tend to get angry but you feel sad. Notice when your sadness has an element of feeling "not being good enough" or "insufficient for what is needed." This may indicate an underlying feeling of shame.

- Notice the impact that discovering bundled feelings has on your thinking and feelings. Most likely you will feel more alive and see more options.

Practice 3: Spend time in good light

Soak up the morning light. Natural light is best in the morning, although beneficial at any time. Make time everyday to be outside. Make sure you have ample lighting in your home and work. When inside, it helps to spend time sitting or working near windows to maximize the impact of natural light.

If you live in a dark climate or must spend significant time indoors, consider purchasing a sunlamp to help avoid Seasonal Affective Disorder (SAD). Experiment with different lighting in your office and home: soft lamps, lights with dimmer switches, and even a variety of bulbs to bring about different light and tonal energy. Notice which ones you gravitate toward and which combinations relax your mind and body.

Practice 4: Practice mindful meditation

A growing body of literature documents the positive impact of mindful meditation. There are many resources and different forms this can take. Whatever meditation practice you choose, they all include the basic notion of becoming still and present. This quiets the mind and opens one up of a broader, deeper intelligence that all humans share. Keys to success include becoming quiet, staying alert in an upright position with intention and attention. Often meditation begins with noticing the breath or the rhythm of your breathing. This quiets and opens the mind and the heart. This sounds simple, but it can be challenging to stop the chatter of the mind with stillness and focus on the body. Often one experiences peace and an expansive sense of being.

Meditation has proven to be helpful for our physical as well as our emotional and spiritual well being. Meditation can be used simply to quiet the mind and renew the mind and spirit or it can be used for different specific reasons.

Some meditation practices focus on

- Physical healing

- Emotional healing

- Building one's intuitive capacity

- Improving relationships

- Letting go of the past

- Deepening spiritual awareness

Practices to Experience Healthy Shame

*Because of its preverbal origins, shame is difficult
to define. It is a healthy human feeling that can become a
true sickness of the soul. . . There are two forms of shame: innate shame
and toxic/life-destroying shame. When shame is toxic,
it is an excruciatingly internal experience of unexpected exposure.
It is a deep wound felt primarily from the inside.*

*Healthy shame lets us know that we are limited. It tells
us that to be human is to be limited.*

*Healthy shame is an emotion that teaches us about
our limits [and] teaches us humility.*

John Bradshaw, *Healing the Shame That Binds You*

*People with too little shame are literally "shameless – they have less
shame than they need to live comfortably in the world. . . . Shame-
deficient people are not really free at all because they are unable to
make good choices about respecting the boundaries of others. . . . They
may not accept social rules and thus violate them, . . . they may have
difficulty connecting deeply with others, . . . and they have trouble putting
themselves in another person's shoes.*

Ronald and Patricia Potter-Efron, *Letting Go Of Shame*

We learn shame in our families at an early age, as early as our preverbal
development. Shame is carried from one generation to the next by sending

the strong message that we are capable of great things and it is essential we live up to this responsibility or we will bring shame upon ourselves and our families. At an early age, children develop an ideal image of whom they could and should be. Often this image is laced with perfection that sets a standard that is often difficult to meet. When this ideal is not met, the child, and later the adult, develops a self-image that they are never good enough. At worst, this message can generate feelings of being unworthy and defective and a belief that we have to work harder so people do not see that we are frauds.

Yet as Bradshaw and the Potter-Efrons point out, healthy shame plays an important role in human relationships and in the development of proper humility. Because shame is an uncomfortable and often painful emotion, people often try to escape it through drugs or denial. To be honest and fully responsible human beings, however, we need to be able to recognize and manage our feelings of shame. The following exercises can help you do this.

Practice 1: Practice asking yourself how you contributed to a difficult situation and ask for feedback

It is challenging to be aware of one's own culpability in a difficult situation when one avoids healthy shame that contributes to our staying connected with others and to our appreciating our own as well as others' limitations.

- When you experience a situation in which there is a difference of opinion or something has not produced the hoped-for results, seriously reflect on your own participation in the situation. Ask yourself the following questions:

- How aware was I of the difficulty or challenge involved?

- To what degree did I give the situation serious consideration and notice others' distress?

- What was my experience during this encounter? What did I feel? What did I think? What did I want?

- How did I contribute to the difficulty?

- What should I do now to acknowledge my contribution to the problem in a way that would contribute to positive outcomes?

Practice 2: Practice modesty and sensitivity to others

Humility and sensitivity to others are important gifts of healthy shame. Think of times in your life when you felt humbled in a way that led to greater acceptance of others. Reliving these moments in your mind, notice what they felt like and what outcome or impact they had on your relationship with the other/s.

Practice 3: Practice listening, observing others, and asking for feedback

Without the healthy sense of shame essential to a natural moral compass, it usually takes clear intention and commitment to care about others and listen to them. Practice listening with eye contact when possible. Also routinely ask others for feedback when you have just finished an interaction that had a degree of intensity to it, asking them about your impact on them and what they would like from you.

Practices to Manage High Shame

Shame is an emotion that we learn early in our families. It is often passed from one generation to the next, so a child learns very early to internalize the need to fit an ideal mold that may be unrealistic. When that occurs, the child may be praised for what he or she achieves; when the standard of achievement is not met, the child is shamed. The stated or unstated message is "don't shame the family." The outcome is often a striving to "be okay."

Individuals who suffer from high shame typically work hard at "hiding" or not being seen for who they believe they really are. The message they carry is "if you only knew me, you would know that I am a fake." Shame can be experienced by others in a variety of ways, ranging from arrogance to just not trying.

Typically, such individuals are plagued by internal chatter than is quite condemning. These are thoughts that heavily affect them but are often not shared with others. According to Ronald and Patricia Potter-Efron:

Here are thoughts that shamed people commonly tell themselves:

- *I am defective (damaged, broken, a mistake, flawed)*

- *I am dirty (soiled, ugly, unclean, impure, disgusting)*

- *I am incompetent (not good enough, inept, ineffectual, useless)*

- *I am unwanted (unloved, unappreciated, uncherished)*

- *I deserve to be abandoned, (forgotten, unloved, left out)*

- *I am weak (small, puny, impotent, feeble)*

- *I am bad (awful, dreadful, evil despicable)*

- *I am pitiful (miserable, insignificant)*

- *I am nothing (worthless, invisible, unnoticed, empty)*

- *I feel ashamed (embarrassed, humiliated, mortified, dishonored)*

> *Persons who are deeply shamed have these thoughts with great regularity. In fact, they often assume that almost everybody thinks this way. . . . They are pretty sure that others agree with their self-evaluation. They believe their associates and family see them this way also.*
>
> *Shame steals energy just as it diminishes self-worth. Most people slowly crumble in the face of a shaming attack. They feel smaller, weaker, less potent...*
>
> *The shamed person may also reason that she will have nothing to feel ashamed about if she never makes a mistake. She then becomes a perfectionist.*
>
> Ronald Potter-Efron and Patricia Potter-Efron, *Letting Go of Shame*

For most adults who carry the burden of shame today, a simple mantra that may be helpful is "I am good enough!" The following are other practices to help us keep shame from becoming exaggerated or crippling.

Practice 1: Break the shame spiral

When you get caught in a shame spiral in which one shame image leads to another, use the following steps to stop it:

- Notice that you are caught in a negative thinking pattern in which one image leads to another.

- In a command voice, say STOP out loud to interrupt the pattern.

- Do something neutral, such as get up and move. Take a walk. Go out in the fresh air.

- Say your negative self-talk out loud. This will help empower you by clearly seeing you are not your negative thoughts and noting how untrue they may be.

- Continue to interrupt your pattern by saying STOP again and again if it takes that.

- Call a friend or change your focus in a way that is tactile, like gardening, cleaning, starting a new project, etc.

- Acknowledge something that you have done that you are pleased with.

- Think of three things you are grateful for this day.

Practice 2: Challenge old shaming messages with new messages that reflect self-worth

Follow these steps to replace unhealthy shaming messages with healthy and self-affirming ones.

Step 1: Identify shaming messages from your past. Include any shaming messages you have received from your family, from others, and from yourself. Write them out as verbatim as possible.

Step 2: For each shaming message, write a revised message that reflects the real you and your self-worth.

Step 3: Practice telling yourself the new messages so you are comfortable with them and can access them in the midst of shaming pain.

Step 4: Heighten your awareness of when your internal shame messages occur. Immediately interrupt the cycle and replace the message with one of your new messages. Say it again and again to allow time for your brain to let go of the difficult feeling and allow new feelings to be activated.

Practice 3: Heighten your awareness of shame and diminish its impact

Identify situations that trigger embarrassment, humiliation, or another experience of shame.

- What is the common denominator that elicits these feelings for you?
- In what early relationships did you feel shame?
  - o Can you identify specific incidents in your early years?
  - o How old were you?
  - o Write about one or more incidents where you experienced humiliation and shame, or when you experienced yourself as "never good enough."
- Picture yourself at that age and focus on your compassion, acceptance, and appreciation for that child. Notice how the pain diminishes and is replaced in part by compassion.
- Rewrite this shame script with a newer, healthier version.

Practice 4: Notice how you shame others in your important relationships

Shaming others is a common practice by persons who are easily touched by their own shame. When two people are easily shamed, shame can be used as a weapon between them.

- Begin by noticing how and when you shame others. This is often done in public in a direct or non-direct way. The outcome of humiliation is the same. You can trick yourself that you "were just kidding." Be honest. Listen and learn from the impact your shaming behavior has on the other.
- Notice your nonverbal behaviors that can be interpreted as shaming others. These may include walking way from another while they

are talking, rolling your eyes, or looking at another person with an inquisitive, derogatory look that implies "what on earth is she talking about?" or "what's with her?"

- Practice noticing the impact of these behaviors on others. How do they respond to you when you shame them?

- Inquire about their experience and make a commitment to better understand yourself and origins of your shaming behavior.

CHAPTER 5

Self-Reflection– Developing a Positive- Negative Orientation

One's capacity to bring "practical optimism" to life is recognized as an essential part of life in many areas, including emotional intelligence, leadership and management development, development of the self, and spiritual reflection. Much of research and theory that has developed over the past decade has led to a new orientation field called "positive psychology." A central belief of Martin Seligman, a major researcher and thinker in the field of positive psychology, is that we can learn optimism, given we are provided the skills to do so, which he calls learned optimism. Positive psychology stresses our ability to learn new ways and patterns of thinking that can change both our brains and our lives. As explained by Dan Baker and Cameron Stauth in *What Happy People Know,*

> *You can change the way you perceive things. Nothing is set in stone— not even the way you are perceiving the world around you at this moment. In every moment of life and every instance of perception, there is a point of opportunity in which you can choose how you perceive the world.*
>
> *Many people, however, don't use this power. Some don't even know it exists. . . . It is easy to be that way, given the brain is hard-wired for fear. But there is saving grace in this situation. Here is a moment— perhaps one-quarter of a second—which this hijacking [of the brain] can be prevented.*
>
> *This means that every urge you will ever have—including every*

85

fearful and every angry urge—contains a quarter-second window of opportunity in which you can disengage from that urge. The significance of this is extraordinary.

Writers in this school of thought from multiple disciplines, ranging from psychology, neurobiology, spirituality, and leadership performance, focus on the power of our thoughts in generating and multiplying positive thinking. Powerful distressing feelings lead to powerful distressing thoughts, which in turn create powerful stories about the other that we use to defend ourselves. The problem in this pattern of defense is that it weakens our spirit and vitality for living and it creates a belief system that can be distorted and close the possibility of our opening our hearts and minds for an alternative potential reality. As these researchers have shown, our positive/negative orientation is a powerful force in our lives that can bring hope and openness or a more closed, protective stance. Although both have value, the ratio of positive to negative orientation in our lives is important. It is easy to be positive when we are not being challenged and we feel in control, but our experience tends to vary dramatically when we are being challenged and are plunged into a situation that feels not only difficult but emotionally dangerous to the very health and well-being of the self.

Researchers have demonstrated that our capacity for emotional intelligence and being expansive, wise, and healthy in the world is dependent upon the synchronicity of our right and left brains. The right brain feels the feeling and rates its level of importance, and the left brain creates the language to describe it and act upon it. In the moment, we often forget that the left brain's function of naming is a total internal experience that may or may not be based in external truth and that we have choices over that naming. Yet, according to Baker and Stauth, knowing that "changing your life can change your language, changing your language can change your life. It can alter your perceptions and thought processes. Even something as simple as calling an unexpected situation a possibility instead of a problem can change the whole way you look at it. . . . Language is so powerful!"

The following practices focus on being aware and taking charge of your thoughts, which are always language based. Knowing you have choices and you are in control of your thoughts is the first step to making changes that can be transformational in your life.

Practice 1: Notice and track your thoughts for a week

For at least a week, commit to note your thoughts in a journal or any form that is comfortable for you. Awareness of our thoughts is ALWAYS the first step. Often people will report they are positive people but their emotional intelligence scores or 360 ratings from others tell quite another story. It is easy for most of us to be positive when we are not challenged by another about something that is important to us. This practice, however, asks you to notice how you interpret the world when someone important to you challenges you and the outcome of the conversation or situation is very important to you.

At these difficult moments, notice and record the following:

- What are your judgments about yourself?
- What are your judgments about the other?
- What is your "story" about the other?
- How does your story drive your next action?
- How often do you go back to clarify your story by getting an accurate update?

It is highly predictable that difficult interactions, particularly those seem to have a pattern that happens again and again in your life, are a result of an unexamined story about yourself and the other. Too often individuals in conflict, whether personal or professional, "make up" without addressing the underlying stories. The result is the pattern will reoccur again and again.

The first step is to notice your own thoughts and interpretations of yourself and others in difficult situations. Noticing your own patterns and knowing you have choices are powerful tools in examining your own thoughts and in learning more about your own stories and those that the other has of you.

Practice 2: Notice your negative thoughts and wants about the situation or another person to stop the pattern

To break out of these unproductive and often self-defeating patterns, reflect on the following:

- What underlying beliefs about yourself drive your negative thoughts about the other person(s)?

- What is the pattern that emerges in your thoughts, about the other and about yourself?

Then practice acknowledging that all of us are doing the best we can and practice letting it be. This practice helps transform negative "Velcro thoughts" that stick in our minds into "Teflon thoughts" that just glide away without effort.

Also notice your resistance to letting go and turning your thoughts into "Teflon thoughts." What do you gain by holding onto negative thoughts? Write out the reasons behind your holding on to these negative thoughts and patterns. For example, is it safety, justice, fairness, fear of being judged? It can be a whole host of things. Naming these can give you insight and help let them go.

Practice 3: Reframe negative situations to gain freedom and power

Use the grid as a guide to help you reframe negative thoughts and situations:

- Write a description of the negative aspects of a situation.

- Write out your negative thoughts.

- Write what triggered those thoughts.

- Are there specific things that generate your negative reaction? Write these out, then rate the level of power over your feelings that you give to that specific item using a scale of 1 to 10 (1=no power, 10=absolute power to make you miserable).

- Identify the challenges that offer you a positive opportunity. If you choose to stay in this situation, what benefit are you deriving from it? Identify any positive aspects of the situation or of the other person for you. Write them down. Is there something you can learn from the situation? Does it present an opportunity for you?

Describe the situation	Write out your negative thoughts	Write out what specific things triggered your negative thoughts

Rank the level of power your feelings or negative thoughts have on you in this situation (1= very little & 10 = great)	Write what benefits you are receiving from remaining in this situation, if any.	If you choose to stay in this situation, what can you learn? How do you want to proceed?

Practice 4: Acknowledge your positive contributions

Acknowledging and honoring yourself is the first step in building a positive orientation. It serves as the foundation for genuinely acknowledging and honoring others.

At the close of the day, acknowledge yourself for one thing you did today that is a positive service that you feel good about. Ideally write it down and internally reflect upon this positive experience as you close your day.

This is a useful practice for discovering what actions we take that bring meaning and zest to our lives. Sometimes we overlook the small acts of daily living that use our best talents and the relationships that give us the greatest meaning.

This practice heightens acknowledgment and appreciation for yourself and for others. You may find it also offers guidance and clarity about where you want to place your internal and external resources to achieve your greatest satisfaction in your life.

Practice 5: Stop the thoughts that feed your negative energy

As noted, exciting new research has proven the power of changing our thoughts in changing our brain and our lives. This practice uses clear intention and strict attention to train and literally change your brain. Make it a part of your daily life and expect radical changes.

Don't stress others by sending out your negative energy. While doing so may offer relief in the moment, it is toxic to you and others and significantly diminishes the quality of relationships.

- Practice being aware of your negativity and take time to go within to soothe the stress or excuse yourself from others and remove yourself from the situation until you can be more present and accepting in the present.

- Practice noticing when you are about to complain or be negative in a way that does not contribute to any positive thought or act.

- Choose silence instead. Notice your choice and acknowledge your positive decision.

Practice 6: Be aware of your negative energy

Noticing, which requires awareness in the moment, is always the first step to making wise choices. Without judging or condemning yourself, listen to what your negativity is saying to you.

- Express empathy toward that internal negative energy (your internal chatter). Acknowledge and respect the pain in the negative energy. Allow it without resistance. Let it just pass you by as you would watching a storm pass by. (When your amygdala is captured by intense negative thoughts, it takes 6 seconds or more for your brain to let them go. Allowing yourself this time before acting on it will diminish your reaction and give you more choices.)

- Then take an action that is positive and supportive of yourself. Have a cup of coffee, listen to your favorite music, move your body, change into something really comfortable, pour yourself your favorite drink, play with your kids, play a game of pick-up ball, call a friend, etc.

Practice 7: Freeze others' negative energy and its impact on you

We are composed of energy. Our thoughts, wants, feelings, and intentions all carry either positive, healing energy or negative energy that can be depleting or toxic to ourselves and others. Negative energy always weakens, while positive energy empowers.

Notice the impact that others' negativity has on you. Practice stopping this negative energy by noticing its weakening impact and then doing something different or by choosing to leave when the quality of the energy does not change.

Ways you may notice the deadening effect of a negative environment may include a feeling of being tired or worn out, increasing difficulty in concentrating, a general change in your mood that feels more "down" or pessimistic, or a feeling of just wanting to leave. These effects are commonly most easily felt in our bodies. We may just feel heavy and down and wanting to leave.

When you notice this happening to you, get up and excuse yourself for a few minutes. Take a quick walk and take several deep breaths. Both of these will literally "clean the air" around you and help you feel more energy and more grounded. Then decide what to do next.

Practice 8: Engage in things that make you feel happy

Make a list of 20 things that make you feel good, that make you smile or laugh. Commit to doing one of these things every day. Keep track of how you feel when you do it and when you forget to do it. Notice the difference it makes in your day, your positive or negative outlook, and your relationships.

Practice 9: Practice smiling

Practice wearing a "half-smile" throughout the day or when you are anticipating some interaction that you have negative feelings about. While this may sound "over the top" to some people, research has proven time and again that a smile on our face registers in our brain in a way that changes our experience to feel more positive. This is the same research that has demonstrated that the brain does not distinguish clearly between actually doing something and thinking about and visualizing it, a practice widely used by professional athletes.

You may feel awkward or silly when you start to do this. You don't need to tell anyone. It just requires intention and focused attention. Try it. It works!

Self Reflection—
Developing a Balanced
Self-Other Orientation

The capacity to see ourselves as separate human beings is the essential beginning of the development of each of us. It is also the first foundational step in the development of emotional intelligence. This ability to separate ourselves from our caregivers and realize that our experience may be different from theirs is the first step in recognizing that not only are the self and others separate but depend upon and create one another. Peter Fonagy, a U.K. theoretician, practitioner, and researcher, describes the early life experiences that make up the first steps to developing a healthy self-other orientation in a model he calls mentalization:

By 18 months, normal infants show a mentalistic understanding of desire. They are able to understand that another person's actions may be driven by feelings and wishes other than their own. Maintaining this process is not a genetically pre-programmed maturational capacity, but rather the product of an inter-subjective developmental process.
The child's . . . understanding of minds (his own and others) is rooted in the experience of having been understood as a mind. Having been so understood . . . permits the child to feel safe in exploring the highways and byways of the other's mental functioning. . . . We maintain that the core of ALL mentalised representations of internal states is acquired through internalisations of the caregiver's image of the infant.

At the core of our selves is the representation of how

we were seen. We think of ourselves and therefore others in
terms of feelings and thoughts, desires or beliefs, because and to
the extent that we were thought of as intentional beings.

Peter Fonagy, *"The Development of Representation"*

As Edwin Friedman puts it in Generation to Generation, "differentiation means the capacity to be an "I" while remaining connected." The challenge to differentiation, he notes, is "to be both non-anxious and present. Anyone can keep his or her own anxiety down by distancing from the other."

So the capacity of a balanced self-other orientation begins in infancy and is a powerful factor in the development of emotional intelligence and healthy relationships throughout our lives. The ideal is to be able to easily recognize our own experience and identify what we feel, think, and want and as well as to notice what others are thinking, feeling, and wanting. A clear definition of healthy differentiation is being able to notice the self and the other and to maintain an emotional connection with the other person even when we are feeling distressed.

Because one's orientation is developed in early life relationships, the degree of balance can vary dramatically between individuals. The tendency to focus more on ourselves or on the other affects how we see the world and respond to relationships. The goal is to move to a balance where we are aware of our own and the other person's experience and honor both. When that is possible, we are able to be open, tolerant, curious, grounded, and wise in our relationships.

People who are more other-focused typically have grown up in families or situations where their well being required that they were aware and sensitive to the world around them and where developing their own "voice" was not nurtured. The result is when stressed or challenged, these other-oriented persons tend to see the problem as outside of themselves, which can result in blaming others and taking the role of "fixing" the situation without

acknowledging their own contribution to it. This lack of identifying their own role in their own experience creates an important gap in critical information needed to make wise choices.

People who are self-focused, on the other hand, have often grown up in families where they were taught that they were special in some way (whether positive or negative) that could make an impact or difference in the family (for better or for worse). As an adult, this orientation results in a tendency to take on responsibility for themselves and for others that is not theirs to take. When things go wrong, especially within relationships, such individuals tend to see it their "job" to make things right. The resulting imbalance within relationships can become very painful over time and deplete our emotional vitality.

The good news is that, whatever our earlier experiences and patterns, we do have a choice. Whatever our self-other focus, we can move toward creating balance today. It just takes intention and attention with disciplined practice. The following practices can help us develop a more balanced and healthy self-other orientation.

Practices to Increase Focus on Self

When we focus primarily on the other, we leave ourselves out of the equation and, by essentially blocking out half of our experience, miss valuable information. Not placing enough value on ourselves can lead to a tendency to take care of others and to encourage their dependency on us. Such relationships can easily lack healthy reciprocity and lead to a sense of aloneness and even emotional depletion because of the imbalance in the relationship.

Practice 1: Practice acknowledging yourself

This sounds so simple, yet if you focus primarily on the world around you, acknowledging yourself may feel awkward or even self-centered. When you acknowledge and value yourself, others will do the same. Try the following practices to help you do this:

- Look at yourself in the mirror in the morning and say aloud, "Good morning, how are you today?"

- Express appreciation for one thing about how you look today.

- Acknowledge the commitment, values, and energy you are putting into something you are doing now (your work, a project, family members, your home, etc.).

- Make a physical space around you (your office, a specific room, desk, home) that is comfortable and feels particularly good for you.

- Create simple, supportive affirmations such as the following and repeat them often:
  - o I am good enough.
  - o I am courageous.
  - o I am confident.

- o I am powerful.
- o I am gentle.
- o I am creative.
- o I am attractive.
- o I am trustworthy.
- o I am honorable.
- o I am full of vitality.
- o I am fully engaged in this world
- o I appreciate the gifts I have been given.

Practice 2: Practice letting others contribute

For those of us who tend to take responsibility for others' happiness or problems, the following practices can help us learn to step back and allow others to share responsibility for and contribute to our relationships and problem solving.

- Do you usually run the errands, get the coffee, make sure that everything is in its place, take care of others? Make a note of the many ways you do such things daily. What do you do? When?

- Decide which of these you plan to let go of. Start with something easy so you stick to your commitment.

- Tell one or two people about this decision and ask them to take over a given task that will help you.

Practice 3: Identify what is important to you

Make a list of what is most important to you, of what gives you life and
energy. This list must focus just on you, not on others or what you do for
others. It can also include what you value about yourself, whether you attend
to this or not. If your typical response is to think about others, this exercise
may be more challenging, but remember to make the list just about what is
important to you.

- Make a list of what is important to you. For example, you might include
  your faith, physical strength, accomplishments, traveling, having quiet time,
  creative self-expression, being flexible and resilient, playing or having fun,
  winning, or close friendships, to suggest just a few.

- Go over your list and prioritize the items in it, forcing yourself to rank them
  from number one in importance and continuing down the list.

- Identify at least one action you will take for each of the top priorities on your
  list. Write down what will you do and when. This is a commitment to focus
  on yourself and care for yourself.

- Look at your list and identify how much of your energy and time you currently
  spend on them. Is there something in the top five items on your list that you
  are neglecting right now? If so, take a moment to contemplate what that
  means for you and how you can dedicate more energy to this priority. What
  action can you take right now?

Practice 4: Identify core messages that taught you to focus on others rather than yourself

The tendency to focus more on others than ourselves is usually a result of core messages we received early in life. The following steps can help you better understand what those messages were and how to move beyond them to develop a healthier self-other orientation.

- Write down these messages you learned early in life. These may or may not have not been stated verbally, but were clear to you as a child. Examples might be "You are being selfish" or "You need to think about others and not just yourself" or such behaviors as giving you recognition only when you were attending to others' needs or doing something for others.

- Identify key relationships and situations where these messages get acted out today. (Typically the higher the stress, the more we focus on the other).

- Identify key relationships and situations that are important to you in which you may put most of your energy on pleasing the other person, making sure they have what they need before you can think about yourself.

- Notice a pattern that you may have with one or two individuals in which your role is taking care of them first and foremost and where they do not reciprocate the same level of taking care toward you.

- Select one pattern or action that you often do but is not healthy for you. Make a commitment to stop. If this is a routine action or pattern that others expect of you (and it may well be), let others know you are making this change. Stick to your commitment for a week. Then reflect on its impact on you.

Practice 5: At work, identify what you want and why

First, focus on what you need to be effective in your work. What do you need to do for yourself?

Then focus on the situation, the team, your boss, your direct reports or others, asking yourself the following:

- What do you need from others?

- Can you ask them directly for what you need? Is this difficult?

- If yes, prepare what you plan to say then commit to following through.

- How did the other person respond to you? How did it work for you?

- What was your experience like for you in the moment when you were asking for what you need?

Practice 6: Notice the impact others have on you

In this exercise, focus only on you:

- Notice your feelings and your thoughts about you, not others.

- Notice what is positive for you. Notice what is negative for you.

- Practice noticing the impact others have on you, focusing only on yourself for one week or month. Attend to each relationship and the interactions you have with them.

- Select the people or interactions that feel best to you. Identify what happens in these relationships that is good for you. Explore how you can extend and expand these types of relationships.

Practice 7: Notice when you are feeling like a victim

When your life seems unfair or you feel that others are taking advantage of you, ask yourself the following:

- What is the nature of this relationship? What is the pattern of interaction with this person?

- Who are you giving your power to?

- How can you interrupt this pattern and make another choice that reduces your dependence upon the other person? For example, it might be helpful to say out loud the feeling and thoughts you are having. Listen carefully to yourself to hear how true your words are for you. Then identify one thing you can do on your own initiative that will be empowering. This may be doing something, going somewhere, writing in your journal, or other actions. The key is to separate yourself from your current cycle of feelings and thoughts. You might make a list of what you know you are really good at or of what you are grateful for, keeping the focus on you alone and your choices. You may also want to identify and write down specific statements you can repeat to yourself again and again until you break the cycle you are in. These can be something like "I am capable."

Practice 8: Notice and name your experience with appreciation

Often individuals who are more other-oriented tend to be more aware of the other than themselves. Separating yourself from the other with a commitment to notice and name your experience several times a day is perhaps the most simple and powerful means to increase awareness and appreciation of yourself.

Reflect on something that you know will add quality and zest to your life that remains an unmet need. What is it? Make a commitment to yourself to act on this in some way. It can be a small step and totally private to you. For example, I love beauty and plants, and creating beauty around me with living plants is calming and life-giving for me.

The result will be a greater awareness of your own experience and an increased zest for living.

Practice 9: Manage appreciation and respect for yourself

Old lessons die hard, even when we are aware of them. To maintain a happier and healthier self-other balance, try these practices:

- Notice when you feel selfish or that you are not giving enough. You may feel guilt.
- What is the message you are telling yourself? Is it old?
- Tell yourself to STOP NOW.
- Get feedback from others.
- Express appreciation for one contribution you have made today.

Practices to Increase Focus on Others

When our focus is primarily on ourselves, it limits our ability to see others clearly and accurately and can limit our ability to fully be present with others and appreciate them. Being able to see and acknowledge others' needs and viewpoints is critical for empathy and rewarding relationships.

Practice 1: Practice noticing and acknowledging others

You may have a tendency to get caught up in your own thoughts and not notice your surroundings or the people around you. Noticing and acknowledging others can be rewarding, for you as well as for them. Some practices for acknowledging others include:

- Greeting others using their names, including family members, co-workers, colleagues, etc.

- Greeting the myriad of individuals who serve you daily, such as the mail carrier, the cashier at the grocery store, the gas station attendant. Note their names and make a comment that lets them know you see them as individuals.

- As a leader or manager, seeking out your direct reports at least weekly to acknowledge them. This does not need to be extensive or related to a work problem. It is simply acknowledging and appreciating your direct reports as human beings. The return on your investment in time will be great!

- Noticing and acknowledging your spouse, your children, or anyone special in your life. Warm acknowledgment creates a willingness to explore life with greater confidence.

Practice 2: Practice listening to the other without thinking about yourself

In your work and personal conversations, practice listening to others with true attention.

- Discipline yourself to stay tuned to the other.

- When you catch yourself thinking about yourself, internally say STOP and shift your focus back to the other.

- Take an opportunity to express empathic acknowledgement, particularly to let the other person know you hear his or her feelings. (Connecting with others' feelings is always the most powerful element in listening and inviting others to engage in return.)

Practice 3: Practice being curious about others and their experiences

Without a genuine sense of curiosity, it is difficult to focus on others with an intention to understand their experience. You can practice being curious in different ways that can be fun, reawakening the curiosity we naturally enjoyed as children.

- Commit to noticing and being curious about something or someone at least three times a day. Take the time to pay attention to what it is like to just notice the other and stop thinking about yourself.

- Make a list of a few people important to you, such as your spouse, child, boss, co-worker, or friend. Be curious about them, identifying some things you don't know about them and would like to know. Just doing this exercise will increase your focus outside of yourself and move you toward an action that can create positive relationships.

Self-Reflection—
Developing a Balanced
Reliance on Each Dimension
of Your Experience

Having the capacity to equally access and rely on each major dimension of our experience, particularly in times of stress, conflict, or confusion, allows us to use the wide array of information available to us to maintain stability and make good choices at difficult times. Each dimension of our experience has value. Our feelings give us meaning and ultimately drive everything we do, our thoughts help us with problem solving, and our wants motivate the action we will take. Ideally, we use our feelings to discern the importance of the situation and its meaning, our thoughts to inform us, and our wants to move us to action.

When these dimensions of our experience are balanced and we can move between them with ease, others see us as stable, practical, reliable, predictable, and safe to be with, as "Steady Eddies." As a result, we can access and rely on each of these dimensions for the important information they provide us. That is not to say that when under stress, even the most balanced among us is likely to have a more negative point of view than when things are going well, but this does not diminish the gift of balance, which is stability and reliability.

When individuals rely more heavily on their wants, the risk is that they may act prematurely without getting all the pertinent information. This is particularly true when a person's feelings tend to be distressing. Quickly moving to action can be a powerful method of self-soothing or managing one's distress. When we move to action as a way to avoid distress, the risk of acting prematurely is heightened. When premature actions are taken, it often results in the action or decision unraveling at a later date. This indicates that important information was missed and others who were essential to successful implementation were not in support of the decision.

When individuals rely more heavily on their thoughts, the risk is that they may get stuck in "analysis paralysis." This is extreme but reflects the risk of making sure everything is perfect and in place before taking action. Gifts of this strategy include having strong analytical skills, strong problem-solving skills, and the ability to identify details and potential problems that others may miss.

When individuals rely more heavily on their feelings, the result depends on what feelings are triggered first and then relied upon. When people access and rely on anger and fear, they may get stuck in what is commonly called a hijacking of the amygdala. When more positive feelings are dominant, they can result in a positive, open approach in relationships, but one others with less reliance on their feelings may experience as too "touchy-feely." The gift of a strong reliance on positive feelings is that feelings provide a powerful and positive guide to everything else, including both thoughts and wants. Feelings provide meaning, purpose, and direction. When reliance on positive feelings is strong, individuals are less reactive, more confident, more resilient, and can be motivating and confidence building for others.

Note what dimension of your experience you want to increase your reliance on in your own work and personal life—your thoughts, your wants, or your feelings. Then try the practices below that apply to the specific area or increased level of balance you would like to develop.

Practice 1: Increase reliance on your feelings

Most of us deny our feelings to some degree because we associate feelings with loss of control. Yet our feelings provide rich, valuable information for our lives and our relationships with others. Practice noticing and naming your feelings. You can choose to express them or not. If noticing and naming your feelings is quite new to you, decide to not express the new feelings you are opening up yourself to. Your decision to notice and name them without expressing them may give you a greater sense of safety and increase your ability to notice and name.

As an initial practice, commit to noticing and naming your feelings several times in a day, perhaps when you get up in the morning, mid-morning, mid-afternoon, and at the end of the day. Notice the range of feelings you report to yourself. As you continue in this practice, allow yourself time to be with a feeling for a short while to explore if there are any hidden feelings underneath what you initially experienced. This discovery process can provide valuable information.

Practice 2: Increase reliance on your wants

Some of us have difficulty defining our wants or we focus on others' wants rather than our own. Practice noticing and naming what you want. Notice the degree to which your wants are positive or negative. Notice the degree to which you feel capable or empowered to make what you want come true.

A simple yet powerful morning exercise is to write brief answers to each of the following:

For this day . . .

- I need _____.
- I want _____.
- I will _____.

Practice 3: Identifying and naming your thoughts, wants, or feelings

Using the following chart as a model, practice the following several times a day, preferably when you get up in the morning, at mid-day, in the afternoon, and in the evening:

- Can you identify how your past experience affects your attitude toward work and personal relationships and the decisions you are making this day?

- Notice how your feelings, thoughts, and/or wants define your actions at work and your decision-making.

- Practice this for one month. Notice the patterns that emerge over time.

Date/Time	Feelings— Thoughts—Wants	Action taken

Empathy—
Developing Empathy Accuracy

Empathy Accuracy is commonly called "mind reading." It might be called a sixth sense because it is the ability to "get into another person's head" and involves accurately identifying what the other person is feeling, thinking, wanting, and intending. It is a valuable capacity that can be developed by focused awareness of others

As Daniel Siegel points out in *The Developing Mind*, "the ability to mind read or have mindsight lets us rapidly detect the emotional state of another." This capacity, he notes, is important for several reasons. For one thing, "it is a form of communication that allows us to perceive others' intentions, to understand social interactions and anticipate the behavior of others. This primitive capacity allows us to detect danger." Those with highly developed empathy accuracy are "less often tricked by the destructive motivations of others, and thus are more likely to survive."

In addition to providing us with some degree of safety in relationships, when this capacity is highly developed, an individual can easily understand other persons or groups and join them, where they are, with ease. It provides a powerful base for entering and building upon relationships.

Empathy accuracy includes clearly reading language or words, the tone of voice, the cadence of speech, facial expressions (particularly eyes), and body language. Reading body language, according to *Psychology Today*, can "reveal a person's most basic emotions. Researchers have shown that when watching a body's movement reduced to points of light on a screen, observes can still read sadness, anger, joy, disgust, fear, and romantic love. We're primed to read emotion in every movement."

Empathy accuracy can also be used for more predatory purposes if not accompanied by compassion or caring for other human beings. In *The*

117

Sociopath Next Door, Martha Stout notes that sociopaths and psychopaths often have highly developed empathy accuracy with a finely tuned skill in identifying others vulnerabilities and attacking those vulnerabilities.

The following practices offer suggestions for developing greater empathy accuracy in our relationships with others, at work and in our personal lives.

Practice 1: Practice tuning in to others

Tune in to others to sharpen your intuitive skills. Make it fun by:

- Noticing people around you. Watch, listen, and interact with genuine curiosity about them and their world. Test your ability to sense what they are thinking or feeling.

- Practicing with your spouse, family members, friends, co-workers, your boss, your direct reports, your clients, at the bus stop, at the grocery store, at the coffee shop—anywhere that you see and interact with people.

- Keeping a journal about your practice.
  - Whom did you encounter?
  - What were your stories about them?
  - Did you strike up a conversation and verify your impressions?

Practice 2: Exercise your listening muscles in relationships and conversations that matter

In any conversation that is important to you and has consequences, practice listening with the following two goals in mind:

- Understanding <u>what the other person is saying.</u> Paraphrasing is a way to understand and inform the other person you heard what was said: "I hear you saying that . . . ."

- Understanding <u>underneath what is actually being said by the person.</u> Explore what he/she is feeling about the topic. Human beings have an emotional architecture that is shared by all, regardless of age, gender, or culture. When you are with another person, notice the emotional expression that you can "hear" and "see." John Wallen, a gifted communications consultant, suggests "perception checking" as an appropriate method, such as by asking, "Are you feeling cautious about talking to me this way?"

Practice 3: Practice empathic acknowledgment of others, listening with an open mind and heart

While this sounds easy, it is estimated that less than 2% of all conversations include basic empathic acknowledgment of the other person. Key elements to be aware of and practice include:

- Letting the person know that you:
  - See her/him
  - Hear her/him
  - Understand her/him
  - Honor her/him
- Listening without interrupting
- Listening without changing the subject
- Not talking about yourself
- Asking questions ONLY to clarify what is being said
- Restraining yourself from helping and giving advice

Your job is to be fully present with the other, listening to understand. The impact is very powerful for building relationships and deconstructing conflict.

Practice 4: Practice Listening

Listening is a critical skill for developing quality relationships and continually expanding our understanding and appreciation of the world, our own lives, and the people around us. Yet we often hear what we want or expect to hear. Instead of listening to the person who is talking, we focus on how we will respond.

Building your listening "muscles" as a game

As you walk outside, focus your attention on how many different sounds you can hear. Listen and jot down the sounds or make a mental note of the number of different sounds you hear. What are they like? How many can you remember five minutes later? See how long you can stay focused on listening to the world around you.

When you are walking in a shopping mall, entering a store, or walking down the street with a friend, agree to spend x minutes listening to the sounds around you. Eavesdrop on conversations around you. When the time is up, share what you heard. Who heard the most things? What did you hear that was the same? What was different? Did you interpret something you hear dIfferently? How?

Building your listening "muscles" as a team development exercise

The above exercise can be modified and used in a team context to demonstrate how listening requires us to be present and attend to the other. It can be fun and very informative.

Practice 5: Build listening skills for the family with storytelling

Play the following game with family members—children are good at this, and it flexes listening "muscles."

- Take turns making up very short, entertaining stories with 10 or so important elements each. The storyteller underlines or makes a note of the 10 items to be remembered. After recounting the narrative, the storyteller asks questions to check the others' memories. (For example, if a character in the story is wearing a red dress, the storyteller asks what she was wearing and what color it was.)

- Everyone else listens carefully to the story and then tries to recall those elements.

- See who listened heard and remembered the most. Give the winner a prize or a special treat.

Practice 6: Practice watching others to build your empathy accuracy without judgment or attachment to the other

Make a note of observing others with the intention of understanding what they must be experiencing. Be curious, and make it a game you can use to practice.

- What are their facial expressions?

- What are they feeling?

- What is their intention?

- What are they thinking?

Practice this on others. Share with them what you thought they were experiencing and why and see how accurate you were. Listen carefully when you check it out.

Practice 7: Practice being present with others—watch, listen, and lean in to understand

This practice can take many forms and can vary from day to day. The goal is to practice being fully aware of others. Some ideas to focus your practice on are listed below. Use these or make up your own.

Decide each morning what and who you will give your complete attention. You may select a particular individual or a certain aspect of all the people you meet this day. You're training your brain to attend to others.

Options for your focus might include:

- Notice what people are wearing. Make a mental note of it for yourself.

- Verbally greet every person you meet in some way, saying hello and making a comment. Practice really listening to the response you receive.

- This day, commit to touching base with every person on your work team, work group, or department to say hello and learn something about him or her. At the end of the day, write down whom you touched base with and what you learned about them.

- Look at people's faces and eyes. Look closely to identify their feelings. Notice the color of their eyes.

- Commit to acknowledging every negative comment you hear with a simple, positive empathic response. Notice the other person's reaction to you.

- Notice and listen to the clerks when you shop for groceries, clothes, gas. What are they saying? What are they feeling? Commit to acknowledging them in a positive way.

Practice 8: Practice capturing the essence of what others are trying to express

Practice tuning in to others to capture what they are expressing beyond their words. What are they feeling? What is their body language saying to you?

Practice this along with someone else. Take time to debrief a discussion or meeting or listen to a radio or television talk show with another person. Write out or think about the essence of what the speakers were trying to express, then compare notes. What did you see and hear that was the same or different?

Practice 9: Practice identifying others' responses in upsetting situations

It is often more difficult to focus on others' words and feelings in stressful situations. After you leave an upsetting situation, take time to draw verbal or visual pictures of others, yourself, and the situation, trying to capture the details about the other and the situation accurately.

- Write or draw what you think the other person was experiencing (thoughts, wants, feelings). Put yourself in the other's shoes. Try to set aside what you want and your experience. Just concentrate on the other, seeing them clearly and identifying what you think they were experiencing.

- If you had been the other person, what do you think you might have been feeling?

- Do you have any questions as you think about the situation? Write them down so you can gather the information later.

Practice 10: Get to know others better

Get to know your team members, your direct reports, and other key individuals in your work and your home world. Show interest in them as individuals.

Ask yourself what you know about the people who are important to you at work. Check if you know the following information about them:

- Are they married? In an important relationship?
- In what community or area do they live?
- Did they grow up in this community or city? Is their family here?
- How long have they worked with this organization?
- What did they do before coming here?
- What challenges do they face?
- What brings them pleasure, fun, or love of living?
- What are their work and life goals?
- What is it about them that you most enjoy and appreciate?

Empathy— Developing Empathy Compassion

Empathy means taking employee's feelings into
thoughtful consideration and then making intelligence
decisions that work those feelings into the response. . . .
Empathy makes resonance possible; lacking empathy,
leaders act in ways that create dissonance.

Daniel Goleman, Richard Boyatzis,
and Annie McKee, *Primal Leadership*

Empathy compassion is the ability to feel another person's pain or joy and deeply know what it must be like to be them. It implies a strong connection without losing one's emotional boundaries. While empathy accuracy reflects the capacity to tune into another person and accurately know what the other is experiencing, empathy compassion is the capacity to join the other person and feel their pain or joy with caring compassion.

When an individual's capacity for empathy compassion is limited, he or she will tend to withdraw and disconnect emotionally from others when he or she is challenged or feels at risk emotionally in any way. The result of disconnection can be profound. In personal relationships, this feels like the other has literally walked away, emotionally denying a meaningful relationship based upon caring and trust. In the workplace, this can be particularly damaging when the boss or someone of high influence disconnects. Direct reports often experience this as the boss's not caring, being aloof or arrogant, and being no longer available to be present with guidance and support. In this type of situation, it becomes highly predictable that trust will flounder, employees will experience heightened anxiety and/or fear, and turnover will increase.

Empathy is an essential foundation for successful conflict management trust, employee development, mentoring, collaboration, and ultimately building a high-performance work environment. No positive healthy relationship can be developed or sustained when empathy accuracy is missing.

Building empathy compassion begins with acknowledging others with a curiosity that draws one to connect with the other. Practicing acknowledgment and curiosity provides the foundation for greater development.

Practice 1: Imagining what it must be like to be the other person begins with curiosity

Practice understanding others. You can do this by watching the news on television, listening to the radio, and having conversations with strangers as well as those with whom you work or live. Practice letting your heart feel what it must be like for the other.

This practice begins with a genuine curiosity. It requires noticing and focusing on another without judgment.

- Notice the person's tone of voice. Do they sound calm, energetic, stressed?

- What is the person wearing?

- How does the other person move their body? What is their posture?

- Notice their face. What do you see?

- Do their movements and their voice flow smoothly with little effort?

- Do they seem confident? Self-conscious?

- Are they subdued or do they seem in command?

Answering these questions require that you take time to notice and be curious with an open heart.

As you focus on the other with curiosity, notice how you are feeling. For example, are you energized, sad? When you can do this well, your own feelings will reflect what the other person is experiencing. Allow yourself to feel your feelings without judgment.

For example, you might see a child on the playground who is playing alone with no adults or children around her. You notice that she is sitting silent, looking around her in an unfocused manner, looking sad or lost. Then notice your own feelings toward her. This will build the empathy compassion muscles in your brain.

Practice 2: Acknowledge others around you

Acknowledgment is perhaps the most powerful tool we can use to increase our awareness and caring for others and to learn healthy interactions with others.

This practice does not require that you care about the person you acknowledge. In fact, this is a powerful practice to use with others you find it difficult or challenging to be around or talk to.

If this is quite new to you, a good place to begin is to acknowledge others as you meet them in your daily life. For example, acknowledge the checkout person at the supermarket, the teller at the bank, the mailman, others on an elevator, or your drycleaner. It is most effective to:

- Look at them directly. Look in their eyes.

- Show a degree of curiosity (others will see this in your face).

- Notice something about them and comment on it. Examples of this can range from "great shoes," "you look tired," "it looks like the rain got you, too," "thanks for getting this mail out today," etc.

- Notice the response you get. Invariably others respond positively because they feel like they have been seen. The impact on you, in turn, is positive.

Practice 3: Prepare for difficult conversations by thinking of loved ones

Research has shown that taking time to consciously immerse ourselves in the feelings we associate with someone we love or respect before we enter a difficult conversation can positively influence our ability to be more open and compassionate during that conversation. It can help us listen better and identify with what it must be like to be the other person. This applies to interactions with both individuals and groups. To practice this,

- Take a quiet moment to remember a loved or deeply respected person in your life, someone you feel close to and appreciative of, and one or more specific interactions with them. As you start this practice, give this some time. This set of memories and feelings is one you will want to flesh out and return to over and over again before entering the difficult conversation.

- Enter into the conversation or event that you anticipate will be difficult.

- Mentally track your experience throughout the event or discussion.

- After the event, reflect on your degree of openness, willingness to listen, and ability to access some appreciation for the person with whom you had the conversation.

This practice has proven to be very powerful. It is worthy of effort and a practice that you can use often.

Empathy—
Empathic Interactions

*In any situation, the person who can most accurately
describe reality without laying blame will emerge as
the leader, whether designated or not.*

Edwin Friedman, *Generation to Generation*

The critical third leg of empathy, empathy interaction, moves from seeing
a person clearly and having compassion for them to interacting with them
in a way that is direct, open, honest, and respectful. The intention of such
Interactions is not to only tell our own stories but to listen carefully to
the other's. The goal is for both individuals to be heard, to learn from one
another, and to expand one's tolerance in relationships. The reward can be
great. In Fierce Conversations, Susan Scott wisely reminds us that "While
many fear 'real conversations,' it is the unreal conversation that should
scare us to death. Unreal conversations are expensive, for the individual
and the organization. No one has to change but everyone has to have the
conversation. When the conversation is real, the change occurs before the
conversation is over."

The following practices can help you practice having emphatic interactions
and recognizing the difference they can make in your relationships with
others.

Practice 1: Practice empathic interactions

This is an exercise you can practice at home, work, or with people you otherwise interact with in your day-to-day life, such as a salesclerk or person in an elevator. Identify what you believe the other person is experiencing. Make it as complete as you can. Notice the other person.

- What do you see?
- What do you hear?
- What is s/he feeling?
- What is s/he thinking and wanting?
- What is motivating the other person?
- What are the person's intentions?

Then initiate a conversation with the person. This can be very light and easy or intentionally deeper, but must be honest and real.

Think of it as practice and make it fun. Then watch the response. Most likely you will be delightfully surprised.

For example, perhaps someone on the elevator looks like they are in a hurry, is wet from the rain, and appears tired. An empathic opener uses what you observe and what you can intuit about the other person: "This rain is really tiring, isn't it? You look like you got more than your share." Or if you are standing in line at the bank and can see that the teller is obviously new to the job and concentrating on trying to both do the right thing and move quickly. When you get up to her window, you might say, "Trying to learn so much so quickly must be stressful at times. I'm impressed."

Practice 2: Notice and stop the habit of interrupting others

Practice keeping a log of your conversations throughout the day and record how often you interrupt others. You can also keep track of this by putting pennies in one pocket and moving a penny from one pocket to another each time you catch yourself interrupting someone. At the end of the day, ask yourself the following questions:

- Do you remember the nature of those conversations?

- Did you interrupt more in some conversations than others? With some people more than others?

- What were you feeling when you interrupted the other person? What were your intentions?

- What did you do when you caught yourself interrupting?

- Did you acknowledge what you had done?

- When you caught yourself and stopped, what was the impact on the other person?

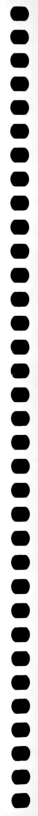

Practice 3: Bring your own and others' assumptions out into the open

This is one core step in open and honest dialogue with others. At stressful times, practice noticing your assumptions about yourself, the other, and the situation. Take time to reflect and be honest with yourself. Often we can easily acknowledge some of our assumptions and not others, particularly those that carry negative judgments.

Practice stating your assumptions to yourself out loud; this is often very clarifying. Then in situations where misunderstanding may occur, practice expressing your assumptions to others. State your assumptions without demands. In any situation that has potential conflict, this practice typically decreases anxiety in the room and the potential for blame. For example, in a meeting that seems to lack clarity, it might be helpful to say something like, "I assume the reason we are here today is ___." Or if you are returning to a difficult conversation to get further clarity, it may be helpful to begin the conversation with something like "My assumption at the opening of our last conversation was ___. My not stating that clearly perhaps led to some confusion."

Practice 4: Heighten your listening skills by observing someone you consider a very skilled listener

Select a person you consider one of the best listeners you know, someone you yourself feel comfortable talking with. For a week, watch this person's nonverbal behavior during conversations with you or others. Notice the following:

- What this person does to convey interest and acceptance of the other person. Write down the behaviors you notice.

- The degree to which these behaviors are part of your communication style. What specific behaviors would you like to learn and integrate into your routine conversations with others?

- Select one or more of these specific practices and intentionally practice it for 30 days.

Adapted from Melvin Silberman, *People Smart*

Practice 5: Learn and practice the essential elements of dialogue

Dialogue is distinguished by three features. Conversations are transformed into dialogue when all three of these components are present:

1. Equality between the individuals and an absence of coercive influences.

2. Listening with empathy, seeking to understand the other's thoughts and feel the other's feelings

3. Bringing assumptions out into the open. Deep-rooted assumptions must be discovered and shared. At times this may be difficult, because when our assumptions about another or another group have negative implications, it is difficult to admit those assumptions to ourselves, let alone honestly telling another.

Practice consciously observing whether these elements are operating in your interactions with others, especially those that seem difficult or strained. Take note of how you feel when others do not respond, using the same rules of interaction. Notice the impact on you and what you choose to do next.

Adapted from Daniel Yankelovich, *The Magic of Dialogue*

Practice 7: Practice "non-violent communication"

The non-violent model of communication includes the four components listed below. To become familiar and skilled in using the concepts and the process itself, select one or two relationships you can practice this with. The practice will build your confidence and competence in using the method. When you become confident and competent in using this method of communication, it can be powerful to use in any interaction that has a degree of confusion, conflict, or emotional energy that may be a barrier to meeting your objectives.

1. Practice observing actions, yours and others'. Observe what is being said or done that is either enriching of life or seems to be defeating. Practice observing it without judgment. When you catch yourself judging, let it drift away as if were being carried by a gentle breeze. Watch it pass by and diminish.

2. Practice feeling. Notice and state how you feel when you are observing the action.

3. Identify the unmet need. What need must be met to move the conversation and the relationship forward? It is important to distinguish between what one wants and what one needs. For example, a person may want a particular outcome to a situation. What one needs is a sense of being respected. When a basic human need is going unmet in a conflict, the problem will not move to a satisfactory and stable resolution.

4. Make a specific request. Discover what would enrich your life and the life of the other (the need) and request a specific action that can help meet that need. This may be some action that demonstrates the person has been heard or the person has demonstrated some degree of empathy compassion for the other person's dilemma.

Adapted from Marshall Rosenberg,
Nonviolent Communication: A Language of Compassion

Practice 8: Use mutual inquiry for feedback and conflict

There is no more powerful approach to building effective relationships than to mutually inquire about the difference between what a person does or says and its impact on you. When this "intention gap" is left open, it can destroy morale, cohesion, productivity, and trust.

Use the following process when:

- There is misunderstanding and conflict that presents some risk to the relationship.

- The relationship has high value.

- Getting clarity and a shared understanding is essential for achieving and sustaining the desired outcomes.

- You have a genuine openness and commitment to increase your understanding and want to create a better outcome.

Step 1: Prepare for the conversation

Each person does the following before the meeting:

- o Do your homework. Trace out your own stories before you initiate the conversation. Consider writing your three levels of stories (see page _**54?**__).

- o Define what you want from this relationship.

- o Define your goals for the upcoming conversation.

Step 2: Open the conversation

Each person takes a turn doing the following while the other listens without interrupting:

- State the purpose of the conversation and the hoped-for outcome.

  - o Describe the behavior of the other (description ONLY).

  - o Share your story about the other's behavior.

- o Describe the impact on you (your feelings, your thoughts, your wants).
- o Invite the other to share the impact of what you have said on him/her and share his/her story.

Self-Regulation—
Effectively Managing Yourself
in Relationships

The capacity to manage ourselves effectively in challenging relationships is based upon our ability to soothe our own distress in a way that allows us to remain in relationship. Trust is developed and maintained only when we experience sufficient emotional safety to be open, authentic, and honest with ourselves and one another. Interacting with integrity is critical to building and sustaining trust. Trust does not precede healthy interactions; it grows out of interacting with integrity.

Trust is something that must be learned. It is learned and practiced only in relationship. Trust is not static. It is dynamic, in an often-changing balance of emotional safety we have with one another. According to Robert Solomon and Fernando Flores,

Trust is always the relationship within which trust is based and which trust itself helps create.

Self-Trust is the most basic and most often neglected form of trust.

- *Distrust is often a projection of missing self-trust*
- *Trust is . . .*
    - *an opening up of the world, not a diminution of it.*
    - *the result of continuous attentiveness and activity.*
    - *often becomes visible only when it has been challenged or violated*
    - *part of the vitality . . . of relationships.*
    - *social practice, not a set of beliefs.*
    - *transformative. It is a matter of changing the relationship through trust*

- *a matter of mood and emotional skills.*

- *is the foundation for true leadership. "True leadership can be based on nothing else."*

- *can never be taken for granted, but must be consciously cultivated through commitments and truthfulness.*

- *the foundation for healthy relationships. Trust is something we can learn.*

From *Building Trust in Business, Politics, Relationships, and Life*

This chapter includes practices for building high-trust relationships, building trust in oneself, building trust on the part if others, and individually soothing ourselves during challenging times.

Practices to Develop Effective Self-Soothing Strategies

We self-soothe ourselves in relationships and by ourselves. Finding effective ways to soothe ourselves when we are alone is critical for maintaining balance and flexibility in relationships. Most of us self-soothe in both healthy ways and unhealthy ways throughout each day. These practices are intended to increase your awareness of how you manage yourself today, in healthy and unhealthy ways, and to offer a list of healthy options for you to consider adding to your life. The focus on soothing ourselves when alone strengthens our ability to be grounded and to be empowered in happy and distressing situations.

Practice 1: Notice how you soothe yourself in stressful situations

Be aware of your experiences and the stories about them that you are creating and listening to right now. Your stories provide powerful clues about how you are soothing yourself. Ask yourself the following questions:

- How you tend to soothe or calm your internal experience when you are stressed?
- What are typical ways you soothe yourself? For example, one person may read, others may take a walk outside, watch television, play games, take a bath, or talk to another person. Can you name ways you typically soothe yourself when you are stressed?
- What triggers your feelings of distress? (Most likely these are situations that trigger powerful feelings from the past.)
- How much are you focusing on the other?
- How much are you focusing on yourself?

Practice just noticing the stories you tell yourself, observing the story play out without judgment. Know you have the power to stop or change the story that is going on in your own internal world.

Practice 2: Identify methods that calm and support you without negative consequences to anyone else

Review situations in the past month that involved some degree of stress or pain for you.

How did you calm yourself and manage your emotions in these situations? It is not uncommon to use self-soothing strategies that look positive and supportive of the relationship but that in fact betray you. This can occur when you consistently manage your emotional safety by giving away your own voice or your own personal authority for the sake of the relationship. When this happens, it can feel like short-term relief but contributes to long-term resentment and pain.

Think about more effective methods and strategies of self-soothing that you would like to practice. You may begin with noting ways you soothe yourself today that do you harm. Harmful methods include a wide array of addictions that we commonly use to soothe our distress or avoid feeling our distress.

We use a variety of methods for self-soothing that we do ourselves, such as reading, walking, etc.

Review that the chart in the following practice that lists positive and negative forms of self-soothing methods. Note what you use today, what you want to give up, and what you may want to add.

Practice 3: Identify familiar self-soothing strategies

Review the helpful and harmful self-soothing strategies listed on the following pages. Which seem familiar to you? Check items you would like to add as part of your daily living practices.

Strategies that support self, others, and relationships	Strategies that hurt self, others, and relationships
Look inside and be aware of your own pain	Dismiss the other
Feel your pain without judgment	Make the other wrong
Reflect on how you contribute to a particular difficult situation	Blame
Use mutual inquiry to learn about the other person's reality	Be sarcastic
Acknowledge your own disappointment and pain; honor the experience without demanding change	Withdraw into silence
Initiate a conversation with the intent to learn and understand	Quit, leave the situation and/or person
Leave the situation temporarily to get grounded and come back when your level of distress has lessened	Bad-mouth others to co-workers or friends
Take several deep breaths to get centered to reduce reactivity	Feel and act superior to others, i.e., smarter, more attractive, or more important
Laugh! Humor can be a powerful tool	Intentionally sabotage others and their goals
Take a walk or exercise	Deny knowledge or any responsibility for a problem

	Practice daily meditation or prayer		Be self-righteous
	Listen to music, reading, sing, play an instrument		Feel and act like a victim
	Eat something comforting		Demand that others change
	Call a friend		Set up additional requirements of others
	Go Shopping or take a great bath		Deny anything is wrong
	Go to a great movie		Coerce others
	Have a good cry with someone you trust		Abuse others physically or verbally
	Join a group that is supportive and helps you learn about yourself		Look to be rescued
	Examine your current relationships. Seek relationships that enrich you and bring you life		Avoid or repress feelings
	Buy yourself flowers		Give-up

	Take up gardening or cooking		See yourself as a failure
	Take a hike or go camping		Blame God or the universe for not being fair
	Write a note to someone you care about		Commit to winning, regardless of the relatlonship or impact on others
	Get a coach		Engage in self criticism - beat up on yourself
	Accept responsibility and apologize when appropriate		Hold on to anger so it becomes chronic
	Focus on what is important to you and take positive action		Stay in a demoralizing relationship
	Declare what you want, not what you don't want		Walk away when challenged
	Get a massage or take up Yoga		Hope for a miracle
	Etc.		Etc.

Practice 4: Identify new calming or self-soothing techniques to adopt

Using the following chart as a guide, write out the techniques that you want to add to your life. Be patient with yourself and be real. Avoid being over-zealous, which just leads to failure.

Strategies I use today

_____

_____

_____

_____

_____

_____

_____

Degree this is helpful or unhelpful

_____

_____

_____

_____

_____

_____

_____

Define any changes I want to make

_____

_____

_____

_____

_____

_____

_____

Strategies I will add to my life

_____

_____

_____

Define specifics of this strategy - I will _____

_____

_____

_____

How is it working?

_____

_____

_____

Strategies I will give up or stop using

_____

_____

_____

Define specific behaviors you will give up

_____

_____

_____

Track your success at this

_____

_____

_____

Practice 5: Find a supportive coach

Create an honest, focused relationship with another who will help hold your feet to the fire in making these changes while being your coach and support. This may be a friend, a mentor, a professional coach. But whichever you choose, be intentional about finding someone who will be honest, who will be present with you NOW, and who is committed to creating a synchronized relationship with you—an intentional dance of learning.

Practice 6: Identify strategies that refresh and renew you

Reflect on what you do when you are feeling sad, mad, hurt, ignored, rejected—anything that feels painful to you in some way. Select three or more things that you have done at those difficult times that helped refresh and renew you. Make those strategies a daily habit!

Practice 7: Commit to laughter

Find ways to make yourself laugh. Rent funny movies, listen to comedy programs, play games you enjoy, and spend time with others that make you laugh.

Laughter is contagious and healing. It soothes, refreshes, strengthens our immune system, lightens our heart, heightens and lightens our energy, and gives us perspective.

Practice 8: Notice self-soothing behaviors that are hurtful to others

When you are feeling discomfort or distress, notice what you do that may be hurtful to yourself and to others.

- Do you withdraw from relationships or go toward relationships?
- Do you blame yourself? Blame others? Blame both?
- Practice noticing and interrupting any behavior that brings you harm. Just tell yourself STOP and make another choice in the moment.

Practice 9: Go within and count to ten before speaking

Sudden, intensive emotions can "hijack" the part of our brain that allows for conscious choice. Breathing and allowing ten seconds before reacting can free up resources so we can choose a response rather than just react.

A similar effective method is to focus on being aware of your distress, excuse yourself, and remove yourself from the situation. Let others know you're leaving and when you will return to talk further.

Practice 10: Practice using a half-smile

Research has shown that maintaining a half-smile actually improves our overall mood and strengthens our positive attitude. You can choose a half-smile when you are feeling angry, sad, frightened, or distressing thoughts. It works!!

Practice 11: Focus on one thing you appreciate about the other person or situation

Practice noticing one thing you appreciate about each person you meet during the day, particularly those with whom you live and work. When this is difficult, watch and listen without judgment. Even an irritating person may be offering you the gift of practicing patience and discipline.

Take time to write the one thing you appreciate most about the other. Notice how doing this makes a difference in your attitude and your relationship in the coming weeks.

Practice 12: Notice your body

Moving "out of your head" and into your body can provide a powerful sanctuary for soothing distress. First drop your attention deep into your abdomen and then throughout your body. Relax the muscles in your face and head.

Then feel the energy in your body. Feel your feet, legs, arms, hands, fingers, torso, and up through your head. Feel the silent energy moving within your body. Focus on the energy pulsating throughout your entire body. Stay there for as long as you are comfortable. This will result in your feeling more grounded and having increased energy.

Pause several times a day to be aware of your body and the energy that propels you. This noticing refreshes and renews and provides you practice in being present, now.

Practice 13: Acknowledge what you did today that was useful to you and others

List three things at the end of each day or week that made a contribution and demonstrated your competence. Watch your progress in beginning to appreciate yourself.

Practice 14: Name one positive thing about your situation right now

Practice this daily, regardless of whether your situation is pleasant or very unpleasant for you; express appreciation for the good things in your life and the lessons it has to teach you.

Practice 15: Exercise—move your body

- Take a walk.

- Monitor your body for tension and practice tension release.

- Join a sports team.

- Learn to swim.

- Take up yoga.

- Learn a sport you have always wanted to try.

- Run a marathon.

- Take up road biking or mountain biking.

- Garden.

- Pick something that both moves your body and gets you into nature.

- Hike, rock climb, mountain climb.

- Listen to your body and respect its natural cycles.

Practice 16: Get yourself a pet—or two or three

If you already have a pet, take time to be with it. Enjoy the love that pets so freely give us. You might also volunteer to offer a "foster home" for a pet that needs nurturing.

Practice 17: Surround yourself with beauty and life

Beauty is a very individual experience. It is surrounding yourself with anything that is calming and nurturing to you. It might include adding something fun or funny to your life or adding plants, color, or good light to your environment. Plants and living things enhance healing. A pet can fit into this picture very well.

Surround yourself with the colors you love, the textures you love, the sounds and smells that you love. True beauty is quieting to your soul.

Practice 18: Get a coach

Identify what you want from a coach. Make a list and prioritize from the most to the least important for you. Ask for references and select a coach. Make a commitment to develop an honest, open relationship with your coach.

Trust your experience. Be open with your coach about what is working and what is not working for you.

Practice 19: Acknowledge and reward yourself for handling a painful situation in a positive way

Think about a difficult situation that you resolved in a positive or effective way, either today or in the past. Note the situation. What happened? What did you experience? What did you do? Identify your feelings and what you did that you are proud of. Acknowledge yourself with a smile.

Practice 20: Reintroduce into your life things that made you happy as a child

In your journal, write about what types of smells, sounds, or touch bring warm, positive memories for you. Name 3-5 specific experiences in your childhood that made you smile, laugh, and feel good all over at that time. What was the essence of these experiences? How can you create them in your life now?

Practices to Build High-Trust Relationships

The way to build authentic trust is to trust.

Trust is a skill learned over time so, like a well-trained athlete, one makes the right moves, usually without much reflection.

Trust is dynamic. . . . It is part of the vitality [of] relationships. . . . It involves personal responsibility, commitment, and change.

Trust is a social practice, not a set of beliefs.

Self-trust is the most basic and most often neglected form of trust.

True leadership, whatever else it may be, can be based on nothing less than trust.

Robert Solomon and Fernando Flores, *Building Trust*

We are emotional beings in the world. As stated earlier, our emotions literally guide our interpretation of ourselves and our world and the choices we make. Managing our emotional safety is a moment-to-moment process for every human being. The greater sense of safety we experience, the more open we are and the more able we are to trust, take risks, recover, and participate fully in relationships. As our emotional safety erodes, we lose trust and tend to pull away from others to protect ourselves. The impact of this is closing ourselves off to the world around us, reducing our tolerance, and restricting our ability to fully experience ourselves and the world.

Trust is the name we give to the dynamic process that allows us to be in relationship in ways that give us wisdom. At times it is wise to trust, and at other times it is wise to be cautious. As Solomon and Flores describe the process of building authentic trust, it is the dynamic process itself that builds trust. It is an emotional action, not a static position.

Trust is fundamental to developing emotional intelligence and expanding our ability to remain open and respond in healthy ways, even in the most trying situations. The following practices offer different ways of staying present and guiding one's capacity for building trust.

Practice 1: Notice your level of trust in relationships that are important to achieving your high-priority goals

Make a list of individuals who are important in achieving your life goals (personally and professionally). On a scale from 1-10 (1 the lowest and 10 the highest), rate the importance each has in your life. Using the same rating scale, rate your level of trust in the individuals. Finally, rate your level of trust in yourself in each relationship.

Individual's name	Impor-tance rating (1-10)	Trust in the person (1-10)	Trust in self in this relation-ship (1-10)

Write your story about each person you named above. What is it about them that you do not trust? Or what about this person makes it easy to trust them? Did you rate trust in yourself high in this relationship? If not, describe what diminishes your trust in yourself. What triggers your mistrust? When mistrust is triggered, what do you do?

Practice 2: Learn how to use different decision-making options effectively at different times

It is easy to get caught in the cycle of swinging between autocratic decision-making and consensual decision-making. When an organization values participative management, it often errs on the side of inviting everyone to participate in everything. Then when the process becomes laborious and frustrations soar, leaders may give up and abdicate responsibility for decisions or they may move back to an autocratic process. When this happens, it is extremely difficult for those left trying to make something work and reduces trust throughout the organization.

There are appropriate times to use autocratic and consensual decision-making. More often, however, consultative decision-making is the best approach, especially when the outcome will affect many people and no one individual has all of the information required to make the best decision.

Using consultative decision-making can be a powerful tool for building trust in others and in oneself. In this type of decision-making, the leader makes the decision after authentic consultation with others. The leader then makes the decision and communicates the decision and the reasons the decision was made to others.

Staying in touch to learn the impact the decision has on others and then acknowledging that impact is the last critical step. This communication and acknowledgement will build trust in you and the organization and others will be more receptive to offering their honest input in the future.

Practice 3: Practice conversations that foster high trust

Practice the following four key elements that will foster trust in any difficult interaction:

1) <u>Observe what is actually happening (behavior).</u>

Take time to be as present as possible, focusing on the specifics of what is happening now.

2) <u>Notice what you feel as you observe the behavior.</u>

This is just noticing and naming your feelings. You may or may not share your feelings at this point, but you are informed by them. If you choose to share them, share only the feelings without attribution or any implication that the other is responsible for your feelings.

3) <u>State what you need from the other person that would make life better.</u>

There may be a significant difference between what you want and what you need. Separating wants from needs is important. When we lead with a human need versus a specific want, it invites the other person's understanding and empathy and they are far more apt to listen. (One example could be the need to feel valued or respected. Another simple illustration is the difference between "I need food" and "I want ice cream" or "I want a steak." As humans we all need food.)

4) <u>Make a specific request of the other.</u>

State this in positive language that is based upon your core need. Ideally your request will be positive for both persons and will elicit the other's sense of empathy and human compassion. The more specific you can be, the more likely your request will be granted.

Adapted from Marshall Rosenberg, Nonviolent Communication:
A Language of Compassion

Practice 4: Create an affirming environment to build trust and a high-EQ team

On a weekly basis, take stock of how you are functioning in your team or among your work group and notice how well you believe your team is doing.

- Ask yourself how positive you are about the team and how your work together is going.

- Focus on being positive and encouraging to others. Say things like, "We can get through this," "Nothing will stop us," "If other teams can do this we certainly can, too—we're smart!"

- Notice the response you receive from others when you become more positive and encouraging.

- Focus on the areas over which you have some control.

- Seek input from others outside of your work group. Ask for input and ideas that will help you build positive relationships with others in the organization.

- Do not blame others, in or outside of your group. If others in your group blame others, openly share the impact it has on you and refocus on what can be done now.

Practice 5: Build relationships and trust between groups

Getting the job done efficiently and effectively usually requires interacting with a host of other work groups outside your own. To help build trust among these groups, do the following:

- Create a list of your group's key external relationships that can positively or negatively impact your output and overall performance.

- Prioritize your list according to your level of interdependence and ease of access to them, placing those with easier access at the top of the list.

- Develop a strategy for relationship building and create opportunities for networking, interaction, and fun with the other group with the intent of getting to know them as people rather than just as "colleagues" or "co-workers."

- When appropriate, invite them to your team meetings.

- Keep them informed of any activity that will impact them and consistently ask for their input.

- Bring your authentic self to the relationship.

- Build in feedback as part of your work routine with them.

Adapted from Vanessa Druskat and Steven Woolf,
"Group Emotional Competence and Its Influence on Group Effectiveness"

Practice 6: Offer simple demonstrations of appreciation

Small expressions of appreciation such as the following can be powerful ways
to build trust in relationships and build individual confidence:

- Send handwritten cards:

- Take the time to write a note to someone. It can be on company
  stationary or an attractive simple card. Spend 15 minutes each day or
  week writing personal notes to people who are part of   your work
  group, department, division or external individuals who have an impact
  you and your work.

- Make the note specific about what they are doing that is a contribution
  and that makes a difference for you.

- This is a morale and confidence booster: it shows you notice, you care,
  and that you recognize their contribution.

- Keep it simple, just saying you notice their efforts and that it's good to
  have them as a part of your organization.

- Once a month, randomly select someone in your work world and
  anonymously send them a bouquet of flowers.

These acknowledgements need to be kept simple. They are simply
acknowledging and honoring the recipient as a human being. The most
powerful contribution you can make to your own and the others' EQ
development is acknowledgement and appreciation for simply being a human
being in the world and contributing to your organization.

Adapted from Kenny Moore, *"Notes from the Corporate Underground"*

Practice 7: Mentor others so you can rely more on others for leadership and support

Mentoring can be a good method for increasing your self-awareness, your empathy, and awareness of others and for building solid high-trust work relationships.

Welcoming the opportunity to have interns can be a good start, as can mentoring someone on a project with which you have extensive experience. The key in building trust is to be committed to understanding your experience as well as the others' and having open, direct conversations in the process.

Often highly independent leaders find mentoring challenging because it requires allowing the other to make mistakes and taking time to help them learn from their errors. These leaders can easily get frustrated and impatient and find it easier to "do it myself." Mentoring takes patience and empathy.

Guidelines for strengthening your ability to mentor effectively include the following:

- Before you begin, reflect upon a time when you were first learning something important. Remember how it felt. Remember this with positive, caring thoughts about yourself during that time. This will increase your ability to be available and supportive.

- Track your own feelings of impatience and frustration. When they occur, take a break and decide upon a time to continue.

- Assume the person is doing his/her best and may be negatively affected by anxiety that will slow down his/her learning.

- Create a process that structures structured in a way that makes it manageable.

- Structure the process so the person knows what to expect and when, including when you will be checking on them to review their progress and provide guidance.

- Structure the process so the person you are mentoring can seek out your guidance and feel safe coming to you.

- Ask for feedback and how it is going often so you are giving your best.

Practice 8: Build trust in yourself and others by keeping your commitments

Many of us find it easy to make commitments to others without giving it much thought or taking the commitment seriously. This erodes our sense of integrity and others' trust in us. The belief that it really won't make a difference typically arises from a lack of self-worth and commitment to ourselves.

To heighten your awareness of your commitments and progress toward meeting them, practice tracking your commitments for one month. Write the following on your calendar, notebook, or journal.

- Describe the commitment—the specific goal and action to be taken.

- The person to whom the commitment was made (self or to the other).

- Date of your commitment and timelines for completion.

Look at your list weekly and note how you are doing.

At the close of the month, notice which commitments were met and which were not. Who suffered the greatest impact of the unmet commitments? Was it you, family members, friends, co-workers, your direct reports, or your boss?

For the commitments that were not met, did you contact the other to discuss the impact and next steps? Did you forget about it or avoid it? Is your response this month indicative of a pattern for you?

While commitments don't always work out, we can usually be in contact with the person who is being affected. Make contacting the other in these situations a routine practice. Notice how your attitude improves about yourself and the other.

Practices to Build Trust in Others

True leadership, whatever else it may be,
can be based on nothing less (than trust).

Authentic trust can never be taken for granted,
but must be continuously cultivated through
commitments and trustfulness.

Robert Solomon and Fernando Flores, *Building Trust*

Being able to move toward another person with a degree of trust is fundamental to creating relationships in which we can learn from others and actively participate in the world around us. Being able to trust others is grounded in our ability to first trust ourselves and maintain a degree of emotional safety that can allow us to risk trusting another person. Trusting is a dynamic, active, learning process that requires a degree of engagement in which one learns from experience in the moment. At a minimum, this demands acknowledgment of the other with a curiosity that may lead to active involvement in the relationship. Building trust in others requires a commitment to be engaged and actively learn in the process. Sometimes it is wise to trust others and move toward them, and at times it is wise to move away. This wisdom and freedom in relationships is learned only through a process of involvement and active engagement that is honest, direct, respectful, and maintains a high level of integrity. Blind trust or simple trust in others lacks the active, honest engagement that trust demands and can set one up to be hurt and used. An automatic distrust can also keep us from the wisdom gained only through active acknowledgment, curiosity, integrity, and honest engagement.

Trusting others and participating in active, honest engagement can be particularly challenging for people whose life experiences have demonstrated

again and again that trusting and engagement with others is emotionally risky and produces pain. For some, these early lessons are powerful and deep and continue to serve as a protection today. So building trust in others must be approached in a step-by-step process that maintains a high degree of respect for oneself.

Trusting others is dynamic and complex, with multiple parts. Focusing on building trust in others is most easily achieved by practicing the specific parts which, when combined, make up dynamic trust. As you focus on building trust in others, focus first on trusting yourself. Grounded self-trust provides the foundation for active engagement with others. Trusting others is a close cousin to empathy accuracy and compassion because we cannot build authentic trust without seeing others accurately and engaging with them with some respect for their experience. (You may want to review empathy practices.)

Practice 1: Notice what is essential for you to feel trust and confidence with others

- Write these needs down.

- Identify specific individuals and situations where you lost trust or your trust was eroded. What specifically happened that reduced your trust?

- Did you talk to the person after this situation occurred to gather information and share the impact on you, or did you withdraw?

Authentic trust is not maintained when the others always responds in the way we wish they would. It is maintained by using moments of disappointment and erosion of trust to open a real conversation.

Practice 2: Ask others for feedback about how you affect them and their level of trust in you

Having conversations about trust is a valuable way to build trust.

- Ask others for feedback on what is important to them.

- Ask them what you do that builds their trust and what you do that erodes trust in you.

- Be honest. Resist being hypocritical. Being hypocritical and "nice" is a powerful way to diminish trust.

Practice 3: Notice when you tell yourself some version of "I will do it myself so it is done right"

This is a symptom of low trust in others and leads to withdrawing from others. Notice:

- When you find yourself "digging in your heels" and need to be right. That means you are no longer listening, you are now defending your position.

- What your internal voice is telling you at those times. This will include strong emotional energy invested in defending yourself.

- What need of yours is not being met that keeps you from being able to listen to and engage the other person.

Can you identify an alternative action and risk taking it instead? Reflect on when your need to be right is triggered and what you do. Practice alternative approaches so it is easier to call upon them when emotions are running high. Below is an example.

Identify what you need that is not being met	Identify feelings, thoughts, and wants you have when this need is not being met
I am not being respected. I need respect.	I am angry at how someone could treat me like this. I think the other is incompetent. I want to leave the situation.

Identify typical responses or actions you take at these times	Identify alternative actions or responses that you may want to try
I respond with anger, stop talking, pull away, and take over what needs to happen	Not pull away but stay, share the impact on me and inquire about what is going on with the other person. Express what I need to move forward with the other person, i.e.,"I need to understand what just happened here. Do you need something from me? Am I missing something? I need some clarity before I can move on."

Practice 4: As a leader, practice delegating to others

Many of us have difficulty delegating to others when we lack trust. We might think, "it will never get done" or "it won't get done right," "he/she won't understand" or "s/he will just end up complaining and in the end I will pay for it." A thousand different internal thoughts could be substituted for these, most of them coming from some past experience. The messages can create a seductive trap that plants the seeds for future exhaustion or failure.

Practice becoming aware of the specific situations or interactions that contribute to your losing trust in the other person or a larger situation. Name the specific issue that gets triggered and creates a loss of trust for you. State your concerns, your expectations, and your confidence in the other with clarity and respect.

Then risk delegating some responsibilities to the other/s. Be specific about what you are delegating and what the other person should expect from you so they have clear boundaries for their work. Build in safety checkpoints that will support the other and manage your fears or anxiety along the way.

Practice 5: Assume the other's intentions are positive

John Wallen has wisely said, "We judge ourselves by our intention and others by the impact they have on us." Coupling this awareness with a commitment to stay alert to our interpretations and "story-making" is a powerful step in opening ourselves to increasing trust in others and to taking action to clarify our intentions.

Commit one week or one month of tracking intention versus impact with one or more important individuals in your life, using a grid like the one below to write down your observations.

Describe the behavior _____

_____

_____

_____

_____

Describe the impact on you _____

_____

_____

_____

_____

Describe your story about the other's intentions _____

_____

_____

_____

_____

Inquire about the other's intentions and compare to your story _____

_____

_____

_____

_____

Practice 7: Take time to get to know others who impact your degree of success

Trust is an emotional process that only develops with active involvement with others. Getting to know people who are important in your life is a powerful step in building trust and provides a baseline of knowledge you can rely upon as your relationship develops and your trust waxes and wanes depending on the situations you find yourself in. The following can help you do this.

- Make a list of individuals who play an important role in your work and who can affect your level of success.

- Rate the degree to which you know each of them, using a scale of 1-10 (1=next to nothing about them and 10= extremely well)

- Select all those on your list you rated at 5 or less. Then think about what you know or don't know about them and what you would genuinely like to know about them in terms of building a high-trust working relationship.

- Take the initiative to contact each one of these individuals with the intent of getting to know them. This can take many forms, from having lunch, dropping by their work area, having coffee, or intentionally working with them on a project.

- As you get to know them, keep notes about that will help you stay attuned to them. Notice how your trust level is positively affected. Make a commitment to yourself to handle any areas of misunderstanding, disappointment, and failure openly and directly.

Practice 8: State your intentions and invite others' participation

During times of conflict and stress, opening any conversation by first stating your intentions can be a powerful tool for gaining trust. When you start talking about something that will have an impact on others without first letting them know why you are talking or what you want, others often get anxious, stop listening, and most likely begin to fill in the blanks with their "story" about you. Stating your intentions reduces surprises and makes it easier for others to listen to you. This can be a very helpful strategy in any personal or business setting, including in meetings where the emotional energy is running high and trust is at risk.

This simple practice can be powerful in building trust. It also helps you gain greater clarity and improves the quality of your message. Examples of leading with your intention include:

"My hope is . . . ."

"My purpose for bringing this up now is . . . ."

'I need to talk about this because I . . . ."

"I really need clarity so that . . . ."

"I want . . . ."

Make sure you are honest, direct, and thorough when you do this. Resist stating only easy, "acceptable" intentions or not stating intentions that you believe may meet resistance. Others experience these as half-truths or "bait and switch," which reduces trust. Give a concrete example of this.

When you have stated your intention and described what you want, STOP and listen!

Practice 9: Let others know you have heard and understood them

Simple acknowledgement is the most powerful tool available for building high-trust relationships. Practice these listening and acknowledging steps:

Listen with complete attention:

- Do not interrupt.

- Do not talk about yourself.

- Do not give advice.

- Do not try to help.

- Do not try to make the other feel better.

- Do not dismiss what the other is saying.

Ask:

- For information to gain clarity ONLY.

- If there is more that the other wants to say before you respond.

Let the other know:

- You heard what they said - simple paraphrasing is useful.

- You feel what they feel - stating what the other feels is the most powerful:

  o "That must be very painful to you."

  o "That must have been thrilling for you."

  o "That sounds very frustrating for you."

  o "How happy you seem!"

- You understand and respect their experience.

Practice 10: Involve others to generate more choices and to make better decisions

When you are under heavy pressure to finish a task, increase production, or get it done right, and your reflex is to turn away from trusting others, stop and try the following practice.

Let go of:
- Needing to be recognized for always being right.

- Having the only valid or the best solution.

- The need to control as a method to make sure you are right.

Actively solicit choices from others:
- Take time to really listen and consider others' ideas.

- Avoid saying, "Yes, but. . . ."

- Try not to criticize, find fault, or say, "We tried it that way and it did not work."

- Invite ideas from outside your work group.

Practice 11: Be aware of how your judgments of others reflect your judgments of yourself

When we have negative judgments about another person, the other person often reflects a part of us that we do not like. We do not see it in ourselves but we see it in others, often with a degree of intensity. Using the following as an example, use this practice to reflect on yourself.

Write out negative judgments you have about another person	Reflect on how you experience that in yourself or powerful messages you received about this in your past
He is lazy.	Lazy is something that was unacceptable in my family. Lazy people are useless. I work hard to not be lazy.
She is unpredictable. You can't count on her for anything.	If I ever did not deliver in my family, I was told I was useless and was punished.
His behavior is embarrassing. I want to keep him away from clients.	Embarrassing behavior reflects on me and triggers my shame. I have done stupid things in my life that I wish I could undo.

Practice 12: Adopt the motto, "assume positive intentions by the other until proven wrong"

Make a note of this in your daily calendar, your computer, your desk, or any place that will provide you a daily reminder. When you find yourself questioning the others' intentions, make a commitment to inquire of the other as a step in building authentic trust.

Practices to Build Trust in Yourself

*Self-trust is the most basic and most often
neglected form of trust.*

*Knowing self-trust is basic and essential if we are
able to believe anything at all.*

*Because authentic trust is an emotional set of
practices involving our moods, it is necessary to be able
to trust our own impulses, moods, and emotions and
to be able to trust our own self-control.*

Robert Solomon and Fernando Flores, *Building Trust*

Self-trust is foundational to being able to explore and actively participate fully in one's world and to actively participate in healthy, mutual relationships. Without self-trust, we tend to give away personal and professional power to others and have difficulty affirming our own value. Without self-trust, it is challenging to make decisions that are outside what we perceive as acceptable. We lose our sparkle and the ability to take pleasure in ourselves. The result is caution and giving others power.

Without self-trust, trusting others is a default stance and tends not to be authentic. When trust is an issue, the first focus should be on ourselves. When trust in ourselves is active, building trust in others will be far easier and certainly more authentic.

Practice 1: Identify pivotal people who shaped your trust in yourself and in others

The first step in building self-trust is building the capacity for self-reflection, starting with attending to your own experience and gaining awareness of your thoughts, wants, feelings, intentions, and motivations. This practice will bring clarity in understanding what and who has shaped your level of trust and identifying messages to build upon and destructive messages from the past that are best left behind. In your journal, reflect upon the following:

- Who contributed to your high trust?

- What was the message you received?

- How does this affect you today?

- Who contributed to your low trust?

- What was the message you received?

- How does this affect you today?

Practice 2: Practice self-reflection

Start by reviewing and selecting at least two practices from the earlier section on self-reflection as part of your daily fitness routine. Then consider adding the following self-reflection practices:

Notice NOW without judgment:
- What am I feeling NOW?

- What am I thinking NOW?

- What do I want NOW?

Let your thoughts come and go. Just watch them.

Notice the patterns of your thoughts, feelings, and wants.
- Are your thoughts, feelings, and wants positive or negative?

- Do you find yourself doubting yourself? If so, listen and then stop, just stop, your negative self-thinking.

Practice 3: Commit to journaling daily

Begin each day with being as present as possible and writing about what you are feeling, thinking, and wanting.

- On a weekly or monthly basis, return to your journal and circle all your feeling words.
- Notice your pattern of feelings. Do one or two of your feelings tend to dominate your experiences?
- Highlight all the statements you made about yourself in yellow and all the statements you made about others in another color.
- Count the number of thoughts/wants that focused on you and the number that focused on others.
- Finally, notice when you were positive and when you were negative.
- Can you see patterns and triggers?

Identify specific areas you want to strengthen and develop your own daily affirmations.

Practice 4: Acknowledge yourself and your right to be alive NOW, just as you are

The following exercises can help you stay in the present and to replace old, negative messages about yourself with more positive and energizing ones:

- Start by noticing yourself and your experience. Notice and appreciate yourself in the mirror.

- Tell yourself good morning and ask yourself how you are feeling today. Ask with genuine curiosity and interest.

- Comfort and respect yourself when you feel blue. Smile and enjoy yourself when you feel happy and energetic.

- When your negative self-talk starts, say STOP. And stop listening. You don't have to listen. Just STOP.

Practice 5: Notice how much you trust yourself in important relationships

Make a list of individuals who are currently the most important in achieving your life success, both personally and professionally. On a scale from 1-10 (1=lowest and 10=highest), rate the degree of importance each has in your life. Use the same rating scale to rate your level of trust in yourself in this particular relationship.

Select one or more high-priority relationships that will be improved by strengthening your confidence, your trust, and your overall belief in yourself.

Individual's name	Importance rating, 1-10	Trust in this relationship, 1-10	Trust in yourself in this relationship, 1-10

Note the degree to which your self-trust in this relationship stems from your past and is not relevant today. Write out your goals and create an action plan for your next encounter with this individual. Role-play your plan with a coach, friend, or trusted colleague.

Practice 6: Identify relationships from your early life that supported high, low, or mixed levels of trust

Our ease in trusting or not trusting others is learned early in life. Those patterns follow us as we grow into adulthood. Identifying early life relationships that supported or impeded trust is a powerful method for separating the past from today. At times we may lack trust in someone because they unconsciously remind us of someone from our early life. In contrast, we may trust someone blindly because they remind us of a safe relationship earlier in our life.

- What were the key messages you learned about trusting others?

- What were some key messages you learned about yourself from others? List them and the source of each message.

- What core messages still plague you during moments of self-doubt and self-mistrust?

- Write out these core messages so that when they occur you can know they have nothing to do with today. They are not real now. This way you can practice just STOPPING listening to them.

When an experience is very intense—more than the situation warrants—it's a given that you are listening to voices and negative messages from your past. These messages may not be real today. Your emotional intensity comes from your past.

Relationships and situations that create intense emotionality need added attention to enable you to be present with your current context. Consider accessing support from a trusted other or a coach.

Practice 7: Act as if you count, as if your contribution really mattered

One of the dilemmas of life is that deep-seated and mostly unconscious beliefs about ourselves sometimes drive our behavior. The outcome is that we create a world that reinforces those very unconscious beliefs.

Many of us suffer from a deeply ingrained belief that we really don't matter, so our behavior and contributions must not really matter, either. I've suffered from this most of my life. So Susan Jeffers' challenge to "act as if you count" was a powerful awakening to my behavior patterns that originated from "not counting." Some of my behaviors included forgetting commitments, being late to appointments or events and not calling in advance, just not showing up for something, and dropping out of something half-way through without thinking about the impact on others. I did not think about others because my belief was I had no impact on them at all.

While we may believe we do not matter, others sometimes experience our behavior as inconsiderate, unresponsive, unreliable, and treating them like they did not count!

Think about the following:

If you really mattered to others, what would you be doing differently?

- With individual family members?
- With your boss?
- With your co-workers?
- With members of your team or work group?
- With individual friends?

Which of your present behaviors are based on a belief that you don't really matter? List how these behaviors have affected the above relationships.

Make a commitment to change one behavior that would reflect that you really count. Write it down. Take time weekly to notice how well you are doing on keeping this commitment.

Practice 8: Notice when you let go of your trust

Be alert to situations in which you have lost your trust in other people. Describe what happened outside of you, what happened inside of you, what you did, and other ways in which you might respond instead.

Describe the other's behavior _____

_____

_____

_____

Your story about the other _____

_____

_____

_____

What you said and did _____

_____

_____

_____

What you wanted that did not happen _____

_____

_____

_____

Options you want to explore now _____

_____

_____

_____

_____

Practice 9: Engage fully with others while you hold on to trusting yourself

Practice trusting yourself and others in situations at work and at home. For example, you might invite others to provide input regarding an important work decision you need to make without losing yourself in the process. Follow these steps:

- Choose something of importance to you that would also benefit from input from others who may not agree with you.

- State your purpose, what you want from others, and how the decision will be made.

- Listen and let others know they are heard and understood.

- Weigh others' thoughts and wants without letting go of your own and your trust in yourself.

- Make the decision.

- Track how it feels to you. Do you feel energized? Deflated? Fearful?

Practice 10: Feel the fear and do it anyway!

Write out what you fear most about yourself, the other, and/or the potential risk of trusting yourself and holding on to your own truth. For most of us, our worst fears include abandonment, rejection, humiliation, shame, physical harm, and loss. For each of these:

- Identify what you would like.

- Identify the perceived risk and challenge the degree to which it is true in this situation or relationship, as opposed to in your past.

- Open an honest conversation with another to identify what is true here and now.

Practice 11: Practice noticing what you want

Take a few minutes each morning to write what you want this day and what
you are going to do. Building self-trust starts with having easy access to your
own experience and what you want. If this is difficult for you, try the following:

- Practice noticing and writing what you want daily. Don't censor
  yourself—just write what comes to your mind.

- Notice any discomfort that you feel with discounting messages such as
  "You shouldn't want that," "Who do you think you are anyway?" "That
  is being selfish," "You should know better," "It's time to grow up and be
  responsible."

- Notice your internal critic and turn away from it. Just STOP listening.

Practice 12: Stop taking on excessive responsibility for the welfare and work of others

Do you too often seem to be the person to organize, plan, take minutes of a meeting, pick up needed items, follow through, remind others, and the like? If so, this may well be motivated by wanting to make sure you are liked, included, or respected. Instead, try the following exercise:

- Practice letting others jump in and help out if this is the typical role you take in work groups, teams, or with family and friends.

- Tell others what you are practicing for yourself and why.

- Notice how this feels. It may initially cause some anxiety and negative "self-chatter." Let it be and congratulate yourself.

- Enjoy it and express appreciation of others.

Practice 13: Recognize situations that erode your self-trust

Using the grid below as an example, examine situations in which you experience loss of self-esteem, shame, fear, or anxiety. Identify corrective actions that you can take to maintain your trust in yourself in such situations.

Describe the situation _____

_____

_____

_____

_____

_____

_____

_____

_____

_____

Write what you want _____

_____

_____

_____

_____

_____

_____

_____

_____

_____

Level of trust in yourself to get what you want (1-10) _____

_____
_____
_____
_____
_____
_____

List barriers that stand in your way _____

_____
_____
_____
_____
_____
_____
_____
_____
_____

What action can you take now? _____

_____
_____
_____
_____
_____
_____
_____
_____
_____

Practice 14: Find a coach who can help you focus on building self-trust and trust in relationships

A good coach can help you identify areas where you tend to rapidly lose trust in yourself, help you with ways to hold on to your own truth, and help you take action steps that offer a positive correction.

Practice 15: Identify how challenging relationships prompt old messages and patterns

The more challenging the relationship, the more likely the relationship touches part of our past and we fall into patterns that we learned early. These patterns can destroy trust in ourselves when we find ourselves in similar situations as an adult. The following exercises can help you quickly identify and break those patterns.

- Identify how your difficult relationships mirror earlier relationships in which you lost trust in yourself and just listened to and agreed with the other. Make a list of all individuals in your work arena who do not seem to meet your standards.

- Write out your assumptions about each individual, including their value to you, what they bring to the situation, what they do that is helpful and hurtful to your relationship and your goals.

- Identify and write down a typical interaction that is a barrier to achieving your goals.

- Notice how this pattern of interaction is similar to past relationships in your life. Can you identify a person or persons with whom you had similar interactions in the past?

- Make a note of the impact your past is having on your present relationships. Initiate a conversation with someone with the goal of pinpointing and sharing how your past relationships may have affected your relationship to this point. Your transparency will most likely build trust.

Practice 16: Listen to the child within you

We all carry our total life experience within us. Some of that experience we have access to and some we do not. The pain, sadness, and loss we experienced as a child have a profound impact on us today. The best way to move forward, heal the pain, and build confidence, resilience, and flexibility is to acknowledge the pain or experience of your inner child and listen with empathy and care.

It is easy to listen to our pain, self-doubt, and lack of self-trust and believe they are true. It is also easy to recognize this pain as from the past and impatiently desire to pull away from or set it aside. Either response inflicts more pain and strengthens exactly what we are trying to overcome.

The pain may be from the past, but that child is alive and well within us and needs to be acknowledged and comforted. This is the only way to heal, release the pain, and be open to the gifts of creativity, vitality, imagination, and playfulness of our child within us.

Practice listening to and loving this tyrannical voice--be it soft or loud--without punishment. Be alert to quickly identifying this voice as your pained child from the past and then stopping to acknowledge it with respect and let your child know it is heard.

Practice 17: Notice your predominant feelings when you lose trust in yourself

When you find yourself doubting yourself, take time to notice the feelings that accompany that lack of trust. Then put the following down on paper:

- Name these feelings. List the feelings so you can read them.

- What are the thoughts and wants associated with those feelings?

- Rate the intensity of these feelings on a scale of 1-10.

Practice noticing when these intense feelings appear so that you can quickly identify your loss of trust. Know that the intensity of the feelings comes from your past.

Express acceptance of those feelings without attachment. Let them glide by you. Let them go away. Acknowledge the feelings out loud, saying you hear and understand they were real in the past but are not real now. Allowing this pained part of you to rest and go away can be very powerful in letting go and becoming present and honest about today.

Practice 18: Use affirmations to build trust in yourself

Begin with the negative messages you absorbed from your early childhood that still affect you today. Write these negative statements on the left side of a piece of paper. On the right side, rewrite these negative statements into positive ones or affirmations. Write your affirmations on note cards that you can keep close by to repeat to yourself several times a day. It is useful to pull these out whenever you are caught in a cycle of self-doubt.

This may well feel clumsy and artificial to you as you begin this process, but don't give up. Practice will make a difference by weakening the brain patterns that carry your negative messages while establishing neural patterns for your positive messages. The following are some examples.

Negative Messages	Rewritten positive messages
You are clumsy.	I am poised and graceful.
You will never amount to anything.	I am a competent, caring, successful adult.
You cannot be trusted to do the right thing.	I am trustworthy and caring.
	I am good enough.
You could and should do better—it's not good enough.	I am responsible for myself and my relationships with others.
You have ruined your life and others around you. How could you be so selfish to do that?	

Practice 19: Reduce your need to be perfect to a need to be good enough

A common attitude that contributes to lack of trust in ourselves is the belief that "I'm never good enough." This can result in perfectionism. You become your harshest critic, constantly scolding yourself for failing to come up to the mark. This increases anxiety, which results in more mistakes, creating an exhausting and unrewarding cycle.

Gaining an understanding of your cycle of thoughts, feelings, and actions can heighten awareness of your negative patterns that reduce trust in yourself. To practice this, use the chart below as a guide to examine situations in which your perfectionism comes to the fore, what thoughts and feelings it sparks, and substitute messages that you can send yourself to stop the cycle.

Adapted from Robert Solomon and Fernando Flores, *Building Trust*

Situation description _____

_____

_____

_____

_____

_____

_____

Negative thoughts about yourself _____

_____

_____

_____

_____

_____

Associated feelings with your thoughts _____

_____

_____

_____

_____

_____

_____

_____

_____

Feeling intensity (1-10) _____

Substitute positive thoughts and an appreciation of yourself _____

_____

_____

_____

_____

_____

_____

_____

_____

_____

_____

Practice 20: Use your journal to examine how your stories fuel self-doubts

For those of us who tend to have higher trust in others than in ourselves, our stories most likely mirror this belief back to us. Examining these stories is useful for gaining awareness of how this happens moment-to-moment in your life. These patterns are hard to change because they are so embedded. Try this exercise to increase your awareness of your patterns and to make some new choices.

When you find yourself giving energy to something or someone by repeatedly thinking about it during the day or night, write out your stories. Notice your degree of trust in yourself and in the other and ask yourself the following:

- Is it out of balance?

- Are you dismissing yourself?

- Are you dismissing the other?

- What action can you take to gain clarity and understanding and move forward?

APPENDIX A

Brief Summary of Your EQ in Action Profile Outcomes

This brief summary is intended to help you pull out key learnings from your EQ In Action Profile that give direction to your own development goals now. Briefly answering these questions may provide clarity and guidance as you move forward.

Overview of my profile—what I learned about myself:

_____

_____

_____

_____

_____

_____

_____

_____

EQ Dimensions that represent my strengths or gifts:

_____

_____

_____

_____

_____

_____

_____

_____

EQ Dimensions that could use attention or focused development:

_____

_____

_____

_____

_____

_____

_____

_____

_____

_____

My primary professional and personal development goals:

_____

_____

_____

_____

_____

_____

_____

_____

_____

_____

_____

Practices I have selected from this handbook or another source that I am committing to add to my daily living:

_____

_____

_____

_____

_____

_____

_____

_____

_____

Practices I have selected from this handbook or another source that I am committed to deleting from my script or daily living:

_____

_____

_____

_____

_____

_____

_____

_____

_____

APPENDIX B

Identify Your Lifetime Relationship Patterns That Impact Your Emotional Intelligence Today

What are core messages you learned about yourself from your early caregivers and perhaps teachers? How do those core messages show up today in ways that are supportive of you and ways that are erosive? Identify these in writing, as in the following examples:

Core messages I learned very early in life that show up today

- You will never amount to anything in life.

- You are so smart you can do anything you want—don't let anyone tell you different.

_____

_____

_____

_____

_____

_____

_____

_____

_____

_____

_____

_____

_____

_____

When, where and how they show up in my life today

- I approach new experiences with caution and fear
- The thought of failing on anything is very frightening.
- I feel like a failure.
- I would like to be like everyone else and not carry this burden with me.

_____

_____

_____

_____

_____

_____

_____

_____

_____

_____

_____

_____

_____

_____

_____

_____

_____

New ways I want to respond to these experiences

- Acknowledge my talents and accomplishments.

- Tell myself: (1) I'm okay. Okay is good. It is better than perfection. (2) I'm giving myself permission to have fun.

_____

_____

_____

_____

_____

_____

_____

_____

_____

_____

_____

_____

_____

_____

_____

_____

_____

_____

APPENDIX C

Your Development Plan

Write down your high-priority areas for development and practices you can commit to.

_____

_____

_____

_____

_____

_____

_____

_____

_____

_____

_____

_____

_____

_____

_____

_____

_____

_____

_____

_____

BIBLIOGRAPHY AND ADDITIONAL RESOURCES

Ainsworth, Mary, Mary Blehar, Everett Waters, and Sally Wall. *Patterns of Attachment: A Psychological Study of the Strange Situation.* Hillsdale, NJ: Erlbaum, 1978.

Baker, Dan, and Stauth, Cameron. *What Happy People Know.* New York: St. Martin's Press, 2003.

Bartholomew, Kim. *"Avoidance of Intimacy: An Attachment Perspective."* Journal of Social and Personal Relationships, 7:2 (1990), 147–78.

Begley, Sharon. *Train Your Mind, Change Your Brain.* New York: Ballantine, 2007.

Bioyatzis, Richard, and Annie McKee. *Resonant Leadership.* Boston: Harvard Business School Press, 2005.

Bourne, Edmund. *Coping With Anxiety.* Oakland, CA: New Harbinger Publications, 2003.

Bowlby, John. *Attachment, vol. 1, Attachment and Loss.* New York: Basic Books, 1969.

_____. *Loss: Sadness and Depression.* New York: Basic Books, 1980.

_____. *Separation: Anxiety and Anger.* New York: Basic Books, 1973.

Bradshaw, John. *Bradshaw on the Family: A Revolutionary Way of Self-Discovery.* Deerfield Beach, FL: Health Communications, 1988.

_____. *Healing the Shame That Binds You.* Deerfield Beach, FL: Health Communications, 2005.

Brown, Byron. *Soul Without Shame: A Guide to Liberating Yourself from the Judge Within.* Boston: Shambala Publications, 1999.

Carson, Rick. *Taming Your Gremlin.* New York: Harper Collins, 2003.

Carter, Les. *The Anger Trap: Free Yourself from the Frustrations that Sabotage Your Life.* New York: Jossey-Bass, 2003.

Chemers, Martin M. An Integrative Theory of Leadership. Mahwah, NJ: Erlbaum, 1997.

Cherniss, Cary. *"Emotional Intelligence and Organizational Effectiveness."* In Cary Cherniss and Daniel Goleman, eds., The Emotionally Intelligent Workplace, 3–12. San Francisco: Jossey-Bass, 2001.

Chopra, Deepak. *"By Looking Inward, Any Individual Has the Capacity to Rise to Greatness."* The School Administrator Web Edition, September 2002.

Church, A. H. *"Managerial Self-Awareness in High-Performing Individuals in Organizations."* Journal of Applied Psychology, 82 (1997), 281–92.

Ciarrochi, Joseph, Joe Forgas, and John D. Mayer, eds. *Emotional Intelligence in Everyday Life: A Scientific Inquiry.* New York: Psychology Press, 2001.

Cooper, Robert K., and Avman Sawaf. *Executive EQ: Emotional Intelligence in Leadership and Organizations.* New York: Berkeley Publishing Group, 1997.

Cooperrider, David, and Diana Whitney. *"Appreciative Inquiry: A Positive Revolution in Change."* In Peggy Holman and Tom Devane, eds., *The Change Handbook: Group Methods for Shaping the Future,* 245–62. San Francisco: Berrett-Koehler, 1999.

Crittenden, Patricia M. *A Dynamic-Maturational Model of Patterns of Attachment in Adulthood,* 2001. Available at www.soton.ac.uk

_____. *"Molding Clay: The Process of Constructing the Self and its Relation to Psychotherapy,"* 2000. Available at www.patcrittenden.com.

Cunha, Paula Viera, and Maria Louro. *"Building Teams That Learn."* Academy of Management Executive, February, 2000.

Daw, Jennifer. *"Road Rage, Air Rage, and Now 'Desk Rage.'"* Monitor on Psychology, July/August 2001, 52-54.

Day, Laura. *Welcome to Your Crisis.* New York: Little Brown, 2006.

Dillon, Ilene L. *"Attaining Emotional Literacy"* (2004). Reprint available through Learning In Action Technologies.

Doidge, Norman. *The Brain That Changes Itself.* New York: Penguin, 2007.

Druskat, Vanessa Urich, and Jane V. Wheeler. *"Managing from the Boundary: The Effective Leadership of Self-Managing Teams."* Academy of Management Journal, 46:4 (2004), 435–57.

Druskat, Vanessa Urich, and Steven B. Woolf. *"Group Emotional Competence and Its Influence on Group Effectiveness."* In Cary Cherniss and Daniel Goleman, eds., *The Emotionally Intelligent Workplace*, 432-55. San Francisco: Jossey-Bass, 2001.

Dulewicz, Victor, and Malcolm Higgs. *"Emotional Intelligence: A Review and Evaluation Study."* Journal of Managerial Psychology, 15:4 (2000), 341–72.

Edmondson, Amy C. *"Learning Curve."* Harvard Quarterly Report on Research, 5:1 (2002).

Ekman, Paul. *Emotions Revealed: Recognizing Faces and Feelings to Improve Communication and Emotional Life.* New York: Henry Holt, 2003.

Feeney, Judith, and Patricia Noller. *Adult Attachment.* Thousand Oaks, CA: Sage, 1996.

Feldman, Daniel A. *The Handbook of Emotionally Intelligent Leadership: Inspiring Others to Achieve Results.* Leadership Performance Solutions, 1999. Available at www.leadershipperformance.com.

Fleishman, E. A., and J. A. Salter. *"Relation between the Leader's Behavior and His Empathy toward Subordinates."* Journal of Industrial Psychology, 1:3 (1963), 79–84.

Fonagy, Peter. *"Attachment in Infancy and the Problem of Conduct Disorders in Adolescence: The Role of Reflective Function."* Plenary address to the International Association of Adolescent Psychiatry, Aix-en-Provence, July 1999.

_____. *"The Development of Representation."* Paper presented at Lendauer Psychotherapiewochen, April 2000.

Fonagy, Peter, Miriam Steele, Howard Steele, and Mary Target. *Reflective-*

Functioning Manual: Version 4.1 for Application to Adult Attachment Interviews. London: University College, London, 1997.

Ford, Debbie. *The Dark Side of the Light Chasers.* New York: Riverhead Books, 1998.

_____. *The Secret of the Shadow: The Power of Owning Your Whole Story.* San Francisco: Harpers, 2002.

Foreman, Judy. *"The 43 Facial Muscles That Reveal: Conversation with Paul Ekman."* Available from Learning in Action Technologies.

Fosha, Diana. *The Transforming Power of Affect: A Model for Accelerated Change.* New York: Perseus Books, 2000.

Fredrickson, Barbara. *Positivity.* New York: Three Rivers Press, 2009.

Friedman, Edwin H. *Generation to Generation.* New York: Guilford Press, 1985.

Frost, Peter J. *Toxic Emotions at Work: How Compassionate Managers Handle Pain and Conflict.* Boston: Harvard Business School Press, 2003.

Gardner, Howard. *Multiple Intelligences: The Theory in Practice.* New York: Basic Books, 1993.

George, Jennifer M. *"Emotions and Leadership: The Role of Emotional Intelligence."* Human Relations, 53:8 (2000), 1027–55.

Gilbert, Roberta. *Extraordinary Relationships: A New Way of Thinking About Human Interactions.* New York: Wiley and Sons, 1992.

Goleman, Daniel. *Emotional Intelligence.* New York: Bantam, 1995.

_____. *Social Intelligence: The New Science of Human Relationships.* New York: Bantam, 2006.

_____. *Working with Emotional Intelligence.* New York: Bantam, 1998.

Goleman, Daniel, Richard E. Boyatzis, and Annie McKee. *Primal Leadership: Learning to Lead with Emotional Intelligence.* Boston: Harvard Business School Publishing, 2002.

Grandey, A. A. *"Emotion Regulation in the Workplace: A New Way to Conceptualize Emotional Labor."* Journal of Occupational Health Psychology, 5 (2000), 95–110.

Huy, Quy. *"Emotional capability, emotional intelligence, and radical change."* Academy of Management Review, 4:2 (1999), 325–45.

Jeffers, Susan. *Feel The Fear and Do It Anyway.* New York: Ballantine Books, 1987.

Kegan, Robert, and Lisa Lahey. *How the Way We Talk Can Change the Way We Work: Seven Languages for Transformation.* New York: Jossey-Bass, 2001.

_____. *Immunity to Change.* Boston: Harvard Business School Publishing, 2009.

Kirshenbaum, Mira. *The Emotional Energy Factor.* New York: Delta Books, 2004.

Kohut, Heinz. *The Restoration of the Self.* New York: International University Press, 1977.

Lambert, Craig. *"Obtuse Organizations: Secret Errors Kill."* Harvard Business Review Magazine, 103:4 (2001), 11.

Lane, R. D., D. Quinlan, G. Schwartz, P. Walker, and S. Zeitlin. *"The Levels of Emotional Awareness Scale (LEAS): A Cognitive-Developmental Measure of Emotion."* Journal of Personality Assessment, 55 (1990), 124–34.

Lazarus, Richard S. *Emotion and Adaptation.* New York: Oxford University Press, 1991.

Lerner, Harriet. *The Dance of Anger.* New York: Harper Collins, 1985.

Lewis, Thomas, Fari Amini, and Richard Lannon. *A General Theory of Love.* New York: Vintage Books, 2001.

Loehr, Jim, and Tony Schwartz. *The Power of Full Engagement: Managing Energy,*

Not Time, Is the Key to High Performance and Personal Renewal. New York: Free Press, 2003.

Lynn, Adele B. *The Emotional Intelligence Activity Book.* New York: American Management Association, 2002.

Macoby, Michael. *"The Power of Transference: Why People Follow the Leader."* Harvard Business Review, Sept. 2004.

Mahler, Margaret, Fred Pine, and Anni Bergman. *The Psychological Birth of the Human Infant.* London: Hutchinson, 1975.

Main, Mary, and R. Goldwyn. *A Typology of Human Attachment Organization: Assessed with Discourse, Drawings and Interview.* New York: Cambridge University Press, 1990.

Masterson, James F. *The Search for the Real Self: Unmasking the Personality Disorders of our Age.* New York: Free Press, 1988.

Matthews, Gerald, Moshe Zeidner, and Richard D. Roberts. *Emotional Intelligence: Science and Myth.* Cambridge, MA: MIT Press, 2002.

Mayer, J. D., D. Goleman, C. Barrett, et al. *"Leading by Feel."* Harvard Business Review, 82:1 (2004), 27–39.

McKay, Matthew, Martha Davis, and Patrick Fanning. *Thoughts and Feelings: Taking Control of Your Moods and Your Life.* Oakland, CA: New Harbinger Publications, 1997.

Middelton-Moz, Jane. *Shame and Guilt: Masters of Disguise.* Deerfield Beach, FL: Health Communications, 1990.

Miller, Jeffrey A. *The Anxious Organization: Why Smart Companies Do Dumb Things.* Facts on Demand Press, 2008.

Mitchell, Stephen A. *Relationality: From Attachment to Intersubjectivity.* London: Analytic Press, 2000.

Moore, Kenny. *"Notes from the Corporate Underground."* Journal for Quality and Participation (2002).

Nay, Robert W. *Taking Charge of Anger: How to Resolve Conflict, Sustain Relationships, and Express Yourself without Losing Control.* New York: Guilford Press, 2004.

Noble, Stephanie. *"Emotions as Honored Guests."* Available from Learning In Action Technologies.

Palmer, B., M. Walls, Z. Burgess, and C. Stough. *"Emotional Intelligence and Effective Leadership."* Leadership & Organization Development Journal, 22:1 (2001), 1–7.

Patterson, Kerry, Joseph Grenny, Ron McMillan, and Al Switzler. *Crucial Conversations: Tools for Talking When Stakes Are High.* New York: McGraw-Hill, 2002.

Pearsall, Paul. *The Heart's Code: Tapping the Wisdom and Power of Our Heart Energy.* New York: Broadway Books, 1998.

Potter-Efron, Ronald, and Patricia Potter-Efron. *Letting Go of Shame: Understanding How Shame Affects Your Life.* Authors: 1989.

Randall, Peter. *Bullying in Adulthood: Assessing the Bullies and Their Victims.* New York: Taylor & Francis, 2001.

Ratey, John J. *A User's Guide to the Brain.* New York: Vintage Books, 2002.

Rosenberg, Marshall. *Nonviolent Communication: A Language of Compassion.* Encinitas, CA: PuddleDancer Press, 2002.

Ruderman, Marlan N., Kelly Hannum, Jean Brittain Leslie, and Judith L. Stead. *"Making the Connection: Leadership Skills and Emotional Intelligence."* Leadership in Action 21:3 (2001), 3–7.

Saarni, Carolyn. *The Development of Emotional Competence.* New York: Gilford Press, 1999.

Sahley, Billie J. *Chronic Emotional Fatigue.* San Antonio, TX: Author, 1992.

Schulz, Mona Lisa. *Awakening Intuition.* New York: Three Rivers Press, 1998.

Scott, Susan. *Fierce Conversations.* New York: Viking Penguin, 2002.

Schore, Allan N. *Affect Regulation and the Origin of the Self: The Neurobiology of Emotional Development.* Mahwah, NJ: Erlbaum, 1994.

_____. *Affect Regulation and the Repair of the Self.* New York: Norton, 2003.

_____. *"The Effects of a Secure Attachment Relationship on Right Brain Development, Affect Regulation, and Infant Mental Health."* Infant Mental Health Journal, 22 (2001), 7–66.

Seligman, Martin. *Learned Optimism: How to Change Your Mind and Your Life.* New York: Simon and Schuster, 1990.

Short, Ronald R. *Learning in Relationship: Foundation for Personal and Professional Success.* Seattle: Learning In Action Technologies, 1998.

Siegel, Daniel J. *The Developing Mind: How Relationships and the Brain Interact to Shape Who We Are.* New York: Gilford Press, 1999.

Sievers, Burkard. *"The Organization Shadow."* Organization Studies 12, 387–404. Reprint available from Learning In Action Technologies.

Silberman, Melvin. *People Smart: Developing Your Interpersonal Intelligence.* San Francisco: Barrett-Koehler Publishers, 2000.

Simmons, Steve, and John Castle Simmons. *Measuring Emotional Intelligence.* Arlington, TX: Summit Publishing, 1997.

Solomon, Marion, and Daniel Siegel, eds. *Healing Trauma: Attachment, Mind, Body, and Brain.* New York: Norton, 2003.

Solomon, Robert, and Fernando Flores. *Building Trust: In Business, Politics, Relationships, and Life.* New York: Oxford University Press, 2001.

Sosik, John J., and Lara E. Megerian. *"Understanding Leader Emotional Intelligence and Performance."* Group and Organization Management, 3:3 (1999), 367–90.

Sroufe, L. Alan, Byron Egeland, Elizabeth A. Carlson, and W. Andrew Collins. *The Development of the Person: The Minnesota Study of Risk and Adaptation from Birth to Adulthood.* New York: Guilford Press, 2005.

Stein, Steven J., and Howard E. Book. *The EQ Edge: Emotional Intelligence and Your Success.* Toronto: Stoddard Publishing, 2000.

Stern, Daniel. *The Interpersonal World of the Human Infant.* New York: Basic Books, 1985.

Sternberg, Esther. *The Balance Within: The Science Connecting Health and Emotions.* New York: Freeman, 2001.

Sternberg, Robert J. *"Managerial Intelligence: Why IQ Isn't Enough."* Journal of Management, 23:3 (1997), 475–93.

Stone, Douglas, Bruce Patton, and Sheila Heen. *Difficult Conversations: How To Discuss What Matters Most.* New York: Penguin, 1999.

Stout, Martha. *The Sociopath Next Door.* New York: Broadway Books, 2005.

Tolle, Eckhart. *The Power of Now.* Novato, CA: New World Library, 1999.

_____. *Practicing the Power of Now.* Novato, CA: New World Library, 1999

_____. *Stillness Speaks.* Novato, CA: New World Library, 2003.

Turo-Shields, Dave. *"How to Tell The Difference Between Sadness and Depression."* Everybody's Mental Health Matters Website (mentalhealthmatters.com), 2009.

Weisinger, Hendrie. *Emotional Intelligence at Work.* San Francisco: Jossey-Bass, 1998.

Yankelovich, Daniel. *The Magic of Dialogue: Transforming Conflict into Cooperation.* New York: Touchstone, 1999.

To Order Handbooks or to Ask for Information

Fitness Handbooks - You in Relationship
300 Daily Practices to build EQ Fitness

Call Learning In Action Technologies

at 206-299-2360